Publication of this resource book was made possible by a grant from the Administration on Children, Youth and Families, Family and Youth Services Bureau, U.S. Department of Health and Human Services (Grant Number #90EV0409). Its contents are solely the responsibility of the authors and do not necessarily represent the official views of the U.S. Department of Health and Human Services.

First Printing: 2014
ISBN-13: 978-1500918514
ISBN-10: 1500918512

National Indigenous Women's Resource Center
515 Lame Deer Avenue | PO Box 99
Lame Deer, MT 59043
niwrc.org

National Indigenous Women's Resource Center

This book is dedicated to Tillie Black Bear, 1946–2014, the grandmother of the movement for the safety of Native women in the United States.

"By doing VAWA these many years, we wanted it to become something that would always be there for women."

—Tillie Black Bear
August 24, 2004

Contents

Chapter 4. Understanding VAWA and Title IX. Safety for Indian Women

Chapter 5. Stronger Together: VAWA—A National Platform for Organizing to Remove Outstanding Barriers to the Safety of Native Women

Acknowledgments

Many people have aided in the conception, production, and completion of this book. NIWRC would like to extend our warm appreciation to the following individuals who have walked the VAWA journey discussed on the pages of this book.

To the leadership and unrelenting determination of the NCAI Task Force on Violence Against Women Co-Chairs to enact VAWA 2013 with the tribal amendments: Terri Henry (2010–2014) and Juana Majel Dixon (2003–present). Words cannot describe the commitment your leadership provided and will continue to provide to the national movement for the safety of Native women—from the midnight teleconferences, to traveling on zero notice, and for your patience in the process of educating members of Congress and national policymakers. The lifesaving reforms made under the VAWA are largely a historical statement to your leadership.

To all the Native women who traveled far from their homelands to share their stories of survival under the public eye and educate Congress on the urgent need for the lifesaving amendments to the VAWA 2013 Safety for Indian Women Title, specifically Cherrah Giles, Diane Millich, Billie Jo Rich, Lisa Brunner, and Deborah Parker.

To the NIWRC federal partners at the Department of Health and Human Services, Family Violence Prevention Division, Family and Youth Services Bureau, Administration for Children and Families, specifically to Shena Williams for her efforts to build a strategic partnership with Indian tribes and the NIWRC.

To the National Congress of American Indians staff attorneys: Virginia Davis (2006–2009), Katy Tyndell (2009–2013), Natasha Anderson (2013–2014).

To the Strong Hearted Native Women's Coalition for the pilot review of the text during the VAWA Tribal Leaders Symposium, held September 18, 2013.

To the first NIWRC Board of Directors for their recognition of the importance and ongoing support of the book project: Tillie Black Bear, founding Board President, 2011; Terri Henry, Board President, Eastern Band of Cherokee Indians, 2011–2014; Carmen O'Leary, Cheyenne River Sioux, 2011–present; Lenora Hootch, Yup'ik Eskimo, 2011–present; Dee Koester, Lower Elwah Klallam, 2011–2014; Ruth Jewell, Penobscot, 2011–present; Wendy Schlater, La Jolla Band of Luiseño Indians, 2011–present; Valli (Kalei) Kanuha, Native Hawaiian, 2011–present; Leanne Guy, Diné, 2012–present.

To the many staff members of the NIWRC who assisted with the development of this book, including Dorma Sahneyah, Tang Cheam, Rose Quilt, Paula Julian, Lisa Brunner, and Annita Lucchesi.

To the wonderful NIWRC consultants: Jacqueline "Jax" Agtuca for her authorship and skills as a political strategist in our movement's VAWA journey, Maria Magallanes for her assistance with copy editing, and Tillie Black Bear for her strategic leadership and guidance that helped this project become a reality.

On July 19, 2014 during the final preparations to send this book to print our beloved sister Tillie Black Bear passed over to the spiritual world. Words cannot convey the legacy that Tillie gifted to our movement. With a deep and heartfelt appreciation we dedicate *Safety for Native Women: VAWA and American Indian Tribes* to the grandmother of the movement for safety of Native women Tillie Black Bear.

—Lucy Simpson
Executive Director, NIWRC

Foreword

In the early years, women opened their homes to other women in need and the children that came with their mothers. In the 1970s, we did this as women helping other women, sisters helping sisters. Since that time, our movement has grown to open the eyes of this country and the world to better understand violence against women.

The role of Native women in the birth and growth of this movement is given voice on the pages that follow. Our role has and will continue to be to connect the violence beyond individual acts to the oppression that gives rise to the violence. As Native women this violence is linked to the colonization by the United States of our nations, lands, and peoples.

As women of the movement we play many roles. One is to understand and reform those laws, policies, lack of resources, and so much more that continues to separate us as Native women. Another is to restore the sovereignty and protections that are original to our Indian tribes. These pages speak of our VAWA journey through which we have made many changes and can learn many lessons.

Looking back over three decades, having spent most of my life as a woman in our resistance movement, I am so proud of our women who went beyond the shelter doors. I am so proud of our movement for safety and sovereignty. As tribal women, as indigenous women, we are helping to create a safer, more humane world.

—Tillie Black Bear
Sicangu Lakota
Rosebud Sioux Tribe
1946–2014

Introduction

The Violence Against Women Act (VAWA) is celebrated as landmark federal legislation that fundamentally changed the response of the United States to violence against women. While the impact of VAWA on the federal and state governments is often discussed, the relationship of VAWA to Indian tribes and the safety of Native women, many times, is not.

The purpose of this book is to provide the perspective of the tribal grassroots movement for the safety of Native women on the significance of VAWA, particularly the Safety for Indian Women Title. Through this publication, we hope to increase the awareness and understanding of the VAWA tribal provisions, review the impact of VAWA upon the response of Indian tribes to such violence, and shed increased light on unaddressed legal barriers to the safety of Native women.

We also hope to provide readers with a greater understanding of the complex political relationships in which the epidemic of violence against Native women is rooted, how the epidemic has developed over time, and how it continues in America today. In particular, this book will provide readers with a tribal perspective on four political relationships that forged a national movement for the safety of Native women:

The relationship of the tribal grassroots movement for the safety of Native women to the passage in 1994 and reauthorizations of the Violence Against Women Act in 2000, 2005, and 2013.

The relationship of the past colonization of American Indian tribes and Alaska Native Villages to contemporary violence committed against Native women.

The relationship of the VAWA Tribal Title to the sovereignty of Indian tribes and enhanced safety for Native women.

The relationship of certain federal laws to the vulnerability of Native women to violent victimization, and the lack of justice services for their protection.

Tillie Black Bear, founding member of the White Buffalo Calf Women Society and the National Coalition Against Domestic Violence, views this lifesaving movement from the perspective of her tribal beliefs:

It is our belief that we are spirits on a human journey. In that way every step we take in our human life is a spiritual act. Every word we speak is a conversation with the Creator. *(August 28, 2004)*

In this context, this book attempts to share the impact of U.S. laws and policies upon the safety of American Indian and Alaska Native women.

Chapter 1

Growth of a Movement to Increase the Safety of Native Women

Advocates for the Safety of Native Women and VAWA

They tell us that in the old days violence against women and children did not exist, and as a result, these words cannot be found within the languages of the first peoples of what is known to many as Turtle Island.[1] Many tribal elders can still speak of the beginning of such violence within their nation, tracing it to an exact point in time and linking the violence to foreign contact. Despite the many differences amongst Native peoples, the link binding all indigenous peoples of the United States is that of spirituality and respect. These tribal beliefs stand in stark contrast to the countries that waged war and conquest against the American Indian tribes. European cultures, and later the United States, were governed by beliefs and laws that held a woman to be the personal property of her father or husband upon marriage. These cultures could not succeed in establishing their dominance in this country without changing the status of tribal women from an honored role to one of a possession.

The U.S. Congress first passed the Violence Against Women Act (VAWA) in 1994,[2] marking the federal government's recognition of the extent and seriousness of violence against women. Ten years later in 2005, Congress reauthorized VAWA with the inclusion of a Safety for Indian Women Title[3] recognizing the unique legal relationship of the United States to Indian tribes and women. The addition of this historic title to VAWA was the result of the grassroots efforts of advocates for Native women and their alliances at a national level. One purpose set forth by Congress for creating the title is "to strengthen the capacity of Indian tribes to exercise their sovereign authority to respond to violent crimes committed against women."[4] In this light, the VAWA of 2005 marked a shift in the recognition by Congress of the seriousness of violence committed against Native[5] women and an attempt to fulfill the federal responsibility for their safety. Since passage of VAWA, Congress has continued to recognize the urgency of addressing violence against Native women specifically in the passage of the Tribal Law and Order Act (TLOA) of 2010. Congress continued the pattern established under VAWA and the TLOA in the 2013 VAWA Reauthorization Act by the historic amendment restoring limited criminal jurisdiction over non-Indians committing certain acts of domestic and dating violence within the jurisdiction of an Indian tribe.

The efforts of tribal women and Indian nations to breathe life into the Violence Against Women Act are living testimony to the dedication of American Indian and Alaska Native peoples to the sacred and time-honored role of women. Tribal women have endured and continue to lead the efforts to create safety and ensure justice for women within their homelands and nationally. The inclusion of American Indian tribes and provisions to increase the safety of Native women in VAWA is the direct result of a movement that began in the late seventies and has matured over the last four decades. This grassroots tribal movement led by American Indian and Alaska Native women has worked diligently in partnership with tribal leadership to inform Congress to reform federal law and policies to increase the safety of Native women. The steadfast focus on ending violence against Native women and the clear link of such violence to the colonization of Indian tribes has built a national movement with strong allies across the women's movement and other oppressed communities.

While literally thousands of individuals and organizations have contributed to the growth of this tribal grassroots movement, tribal women within their respective nations and sustained by their tribal beliefs have anchored the movement. Within the lower forty-eight continental United States, Matilda Black Bear, Sicangu Lakota, has dedicated her life to increasing safety of tribal women and building a national movement for all women. In Alaska, Lenora Hootch, Yup'ik, joined the grassroots shelter movement in 1978 as a teenager and has continued to lead in Alaska and nationally to enhance the response of Alaska Native Villages to violence against women. The story of the American Indian and Alaska Native movement for the safety of women is reflected in the experiences of these two women, whose journey as lifelong advocates for their Native sisters is shared with hundreds of tribal women who are the lifeblood of this movement for social justice.

Matilda "Tillie" Black Bear—Founding Mother, White Buffalo Calf Woman Society Shelter (1977)

> By doing VAWA these many years, we wanted it to become something that would always be there for women.

As Indian women we have survived. As tribal nations we have survived. We have survived because of our beliefs, teachings, and traditions. One of our strongest beliefs we have as Lakota people has been in the teachings of the White Buffalo Calf Woman. One of the first teachings of the White Buffalo Calf Woman was that even in thought women were to be respected. The White Buffalo Calf Woman Society on the Rosebud reservation was created by and for Sicangu women on our reservation. While we do the work within our tribal nations, we also realize the work needs to be done inter-tribally, and at the state and the national level.

Back in 1979, the National Coalition Against Domestic Violence Steering Committee was invited to the Rosebud reservation. Women carried backpacks and sleeping bags and flew into Pierre, South Dakota, and then came on down to Rosebud. It was one beginning of our national movement. Women from across the country camped on our powwow grounds here on Rosebud. Tribal women were part of the creation of the National Coalition Against Domestic Violence. Tribal women also played important roles in creating state domestic violence coalitions here in South Dakota, North Dakota, and Wisconsin.

When the National Coalition was first incorporated in 1978, there were pieces of legislation in both the House and Senate that lost by a great majority. When those pieces of legislation did not pass in Congress, the states began to pass laws to protect women. The women in those states provided the leadership for passing legislation in their states. I remember going to the Hill for some of the first meetings when the national pieces were first being talked about. I went to make sure that Indian women were not forgotten—that there was language in those bills that protected the sovereignty of Indian nations as well as tribal women. So the women who were doing this work, the VAWA legislation, knew that there had to be special language for tribal nations because tribal women were certainly involved.

By doing VAWA these many years, we wanted it to become something that would always be there for women. So as women doing this work, we can't just stop because VAWA has given us the money to do this work. We have to make those connections beyond the shelter doors—that is what it is all about. We do the work in the trenches, but we have to make the connections outside the shelter doors to say, stop, this is how we can stop the violence against women.[6]

On the Signing of VAWA 2013
Words of Thanks from Tillie Black Bear,
Sicangu Lakota, March 7, 2013

Today's focus is on women and the world around them and how the circle surrounding them supported, nurtured, and honored them.

Keeping in mind that today is an herstorical day in the United States for women as President Obama signs the passage of the 2013 Violence Against Women Act. Lilili!

Keeping in mind that it is only right that President Obama signs VAWA on this day. Lilili!

Keeping in mind that the theme for International Women's Day is "Ending Violence Against Women." Lilili!

Keeping in mind that this VAWA legislation will give Indian tribes the necessary tools to provide safety and justice to tribal women from non-tribal men who commit physical and sexual violence on federally recognized tribal lands. Lililili!

Keeping in mind that in solidarity tribal women are inherently sacred. Lilili!

Keeping in mind that we will stand in solidarity in resistance against male violence and sexual violence. Lilili!

Keeping in mind that our work in providing safety and sovereignty to tribal women has expanded beyond the shelter doors. Lilili!

Keeping in mind that as Women of Resistance we will move in solidarity to end violence against women. Lilili!

Keeping in mind as tribal women and allies that the commitment to bring safety and justice and restore the sacredness of women has only just begun; the sovereignty of women has always been sacred. Lilili!

Nugange (Lenora "Lynn" Hootch)—Founding Mother, Alaska Native Village of Emmonak Women's Shelter (1979)

It was always my dream that we would have programs that were created by and for Native women.

I have lived in the Alaska Native Village of Emmonak my entire life, and I am a mother of five children and six grandchildren. Over the last 35 years, I have dedicated my life to working within Emmonak, the surrounding villages, and with the state and allies in the lower forty-eight to uphold Yup'ik values, customs, and traditions in advocating for an end to violence against Alaska Native women.

I am a founder and former Director of the Emmonak Women's Shelter, the only Native village–based shelter in Alaska operating since 1979. Concerned village members and volunteers like myself established the shelter—the second oldest known Native women's shelter in the United States—because we saw a critical need to provide safety for women and their children victimized by domestic violence, sexual assault, and other forms of abuse. We opened the shelter to provide emergency shelter and assistance to victims and since our beginning have helped women from all over the state, more often than not on a volunteer basis and without funding.

The Village of Emmonak is a Yup'ik Eskimo Village with a population of approximately 800 enrolled tribal members. Emmonak is located in southwestern Alaska, approximately 200 air miles northwest of Bethel and 490 air miles northwest of Anchorage. There are no road systems in the entire region—the river is our highway. Our primary mode of transportation includes boats during the summer months and snow machines during the winter months. Winter trails connect villages by snow machine unless extreme winter weather makes travelling impossible. Depending upon the weather, entry into and out of the villages may be severely restricted for days or even weeks. In addition to serving Emmonak the shelter provides services to 13 other federally recognized Yup'ik tribes/villages.

Since my journey began working and helping women in rural, remote Alaska villages, I have seen and listened to countless stories filled with so much pain and have heard the crying voices of our Native women, our sisters, our aunties, grandmothers, and children, often with nowhere to go for safety. In reality, there is no safe place to go in the villages, except to local churches (if doors are left open), inside willows, in steam baths, and/or fish smokehouses (caches). There are no readily available resources and many women and children have no reliable police protection. We cannot simply get into a car and drive away—we run, many times with five children with us as we hide under our homes in the dark, cold, winter months. Sometimes, if we're lucky, we might see a porch door open and we run inside the house, not knowing whom the house belongs to or whether someone is home . . . this we do to keep ourselves alive.

As the founder and Director of the Yup'ik Women's Coalition, I know VAWA is our hope for the future. I realize I have spent much of my life focusing on violence-related issues. Over the last 35 years we have worked hard to create the changes needed so women will be safe. Like so many other women now involved in this movement and our mothers before us, we really have no choice. Domestic violence, rape, suicide, and now sex trafficking are threatening the future of our people and villages. Our people are living daily in peril. VAWA must include the 229 villages of Alaska. We must stand together and build our national movement to end this violence. Quayana Cak'naq!

Continuity of the Movement and
Steadfast Focus on the Safety of Women

The continuity of the tribal grassroots movement over the last four decades is a blessing that has helped to sustain the movement. This continuity of leadership is highlighted by the story of two Native women during the signing of the Tribal Law and Order Act (TLOA) in 2010. This Act followed the VAWA 2005 creation of a Tribal Title and received strong support from the tribal grassroots movement. It was also the result of the support for such reforms by Congress and the Obama-Biden administration. The TLOA restored the authority of Indian tribes to sentence offenders for more than a maximum of one year per crime.

On the afternoon of July 29, 2010, a gathering took place in the East Wing of the White House for the signing of the TLOA. It was not a typical gathering in terms of the personalities invited to listen to an American President speak, the words spoken, or the person designated to introduce the President. Gathered at the East Wing were elected leaders of American Indian nations, members of Congress, advocates for Native women, tribal law enforcement, and many more to witness the signing of an historic bill to create comprehensive law enforcement reform for American Indian tribes. Seven long years in the making with many hands from across the land involved, the TLOA waited upon a desk next to the podium for the President's signature.

All eyes focused on the door from which the President would enter. They watched as Congressional and tribal leaders who championed the bill's passage over many years entered and walked onto the stage. The last to enter and step onto the stage was a Sicangu Lakota woman wearing a traditional dark blue Lakota dress. She stopped and placed her hands upon the podium and looked out onto those gathered. She was silent and the room was motionless and filled with anticipation.

The woman and the blue dress she wore had each traveled different paths to reach the East Wing of the White House on the 29th day of July 2010. For both, it had been a very long, arduous journey to this podium to introduce the Honorable Barack Obama, 44th President of the United States.

"Good afternoon I am Ta Wacinya Waste Win (Her Good Plume Woman)." And then time appeared to freeze as the woman's eyes looked out upon those gathered. It was a monumental moment for her nation and all Indian nations. Tears filled her eyes as the significance of the event rested upon her shoulders.

"I am known as Lisa Marie Iyotte."

Tears rolling down her cheeks, she could not speak and stood still. The silence came again as those gathered in the room felt compassion. Few of these honored guests, each a leader in their own right, knew of the journey of the woman or the dress she wore on this day. The dress had originally been made for Tillie Black Bear, the grandmother of the movement for safety of Native women, on the special occasion of Tillie receiving a Point of Light Award from President George Bush, Senior.

"I am from the Sicangu Lakota Tiospye, the Rosebud Sioux Tribe. My mother is Roban Packard from St. Francis, South Dakota, where I grew up. My father is Nihan Woo Groban from Buffalo Run. He is known as Ruben Cochran. He is from the Ft. Belknap Groban Tribe, the White Clay People. I am an enrolled member of the White Clay People, my father's tribe, but I grew up and lived as a Sicangu Lakota. If the Tribal Law and Order Act had existed 16 years ago, my story would be very different."

"On May 15, 1994, I was living with my two daughters on the Rosebud reservation. That night I was violently beaten and raped. My little girls saw the assault and hid in the bedroom."

The blue dress was also worn on December 6, 2000, on the occasion of Tillie Black Bear receiving the Eleanor Roosevelt Award for Human Rights from President Bill Clinton.

On October 2001, the blue dress then traveled across the Pacific Ocean to be worn on the occasion of an historic meeting of the American Indian women's coalitions and the national Maori women's collective. The exchange would be the foundation of and enlighten the strategy for the creation of the Safety for Indian Women Title contained in the 2005 Violence Against Women Act. It was worn not by Tillie Black Bear but by another sister of the movement, Verna Mato Estima. Speaking before the Maori women, Verna told them of Tillie Black Bear and the movement for the safety of American Indian women across the big water.

"I received treatment at the Indian Health Service Hospital but no doctor talked to me about the rape. I had to wait all night for someone to collect DNA."

On February 25, 2003, the dress then traveled to Washington, DC, for a briefing organized by advocates for the safety of Native women to educate Congress on the need for a special title within VAWA for Native women. While typical of many such receptions on Capitol Hill, this was remarkably different in that Tillie Black Bear led a Wiping of the Tears Ceremony for all those who had lost mothers, sisters, and daughters—Native women whose human journey was ended as the result of domestic or sexual violence.

"Tribal police suspected a local man but no federal investigators interviewed me. Federal authorities declined to get involved because the attacker had not used a weapon."

In October 2007, the dress then journeyed to the hearing room of the Senate Committee on Indian Affairs for a hearing on violence committed against American Indian women. The dress was worn by a Lakota woman, Karen Artichoker, who was called by the Committee to testify about the violence committed against Native women. The Committee witnessed the telling of the story of the erosion over time of respect for the honored status of tribal women within their nations. They heard stories of horrific crimes committed not during the period of Indian Wars but crimes committed in that year just weeks before the hearing.

"A few months later, the same man assaulted another woman. It wasn't until he raped a teenage girl that he was finally arrested and convicted. He was never prosecuted for raping me."

And on July 29, 2010, the dress found itself at the podium in the East Wing of the White House to introduce the President of the United States. It was the same royal blue, with beads and an eagle feather for purity. Those sisters who lived the journey of the dress over the years knew it well. For decades, many believed this day would never come—that the one-year sentencing limitation placed on Indian nations would never change.

"The Tribal Law and Order Act will prevent cases like mine from slipping through the cracks. There will be standardized sexual assault policies and protocols at Indian Health Service facilities. Improved evidence collection will boost conviction rates. And expanded training of tribal enforcement officers will ensure that victims of domestic violence and sexual assault will be met by tribal authorities who understand their cases."

Many in the room watched with tears falling for the woman who stood at the podium so brave and so very strong, and they began to applaud.

"I am now an advocate for victims of sexual violence. I know the Act will help keep tribal communities safe. We thank the President for his remarkable leadership. It is now my honor to introduce President Obama."

As the President embraced the brave-hearted woman, all those present recognized that history was occurring at that very moment. As Lisa Marie Iyotte stepped back, President Obama turned and motioned her to stay at the podium by his side.

With a bright smile, Lisa speaking for thousands of tribal women had thanked the President not only for the words he spoke, but the actions he had mandated since taking office. Just as the blue dress had traveled a journey, the woman also knew from her life experience that violence against Native women must be addressed to safeguard the everyday lives of tribal women. Since the time of her assault, she walked her own path to restore balance in her life.

Seated at the desk, the President signed the Act into law. "It is done," said President Obama laying the pen upon the table. "It is done."

Over 30 years ago, Native women in the lower forty-eight and in Alaska organized to create shelter programs and safe houses. They opened the doors of their homes; women helped women. These many isolated efforts over three decades ago have grown together to create a grassroots movement of tribal women. It is a movement that clearly identifies the acceptance of violence against tribal women today as being rooted in the violence used against Indian nations in the past.

On the day Lisa Marie Iyotte received a call from the White House, she said, "I knew the dress I hoped to wear." And as she spoke from the podium, her sisters, in the Alaska Native Villages, in the Pueblos of New Mexico and Arizona tribal lands, in the rancherias and reservations of California, on the reservations on the Great Plains, and in so many other communities, watched her proudly. Crying with her, they applauded for her and their President. Many who were present knew the blue dress and understood why Lisa wore it on this historic occasion.

Continuity is a remarkable strength of our movement for the safety of Native women. The journey of the blue dress is one beautiful story among many that reflects the strength of our movement that is firmly rooted by tribal women within their respective tribal beliefs and nations. It is a gift from the Creator that since the late 1970s Native women have dedicated their lives to building a grassroots movement that maintains a belief that violence is not our tradition and that women are sacred.

National Alliance of Tribal Grassroots Advocates, Tribal Leadership, and National Organizations

> Looking out from the podium I could see the women come into the hall and knew it was their time and that we needed to do more.
>
> —Tex ("Ihbudah Hishi") "Red Tipped Arrow" Hall, President 2003, National Congress of American Indians[7]

In 2003, tribal advocates and the directors of tribal coalitions presented to the National Congress of American Indians (NCAI) the urgent need to reauthorize VAWA, including critically needed tribal provisions. As a result, NCAI created a Task Force dedicated to increasing the safety of Native women on a national policy level. The Task Force responds to issues impacting the safety of women and response of Indian tribes on a national level, reauthorization and implementation of VAWA, and other issues. The Task Force operates on a volunteer basis and is a partnership of elected tribal leaders and advocates providing services to women. Meeting three times a year before each national NCAI meeting, it reviews and presents resolutions to the membership body for a vote on national efforts of NCAI staff. The development of the Task Force in 2003 marked a tremendous step forward in the movement's ability to impact national policy and legislation.

As a tribal grassroots movement grew from sister helping sister, so did movements in other communities across the United States that worked to establish shelter and related services for battered women and victims of rape. Since the formation of the National Coalition Against Domestic Violence in 1979, Native women have worked alongside women in other communities to increase services and reform the justice system's response to such crimes. The founding mothers of the battered women's movement, recognizing the important role of Native women like Tillie Black Bear, Karen Artichoker, and Tina Olson, were strong allies for the inclusion of Native women not as token representation but as leaders of the national movement. One of the strongest allies was Ellen Pence, founder of the Duluth Project and Praxis International. Ellen helped lead the struggle for the concept of "parallel development"—the approach that Native and non-Native programming develop at the same pace along with resources to create services for their respective communities. Ellen and other non-Native women stood side-by-side with their Native sisters though the early decades of movement building from the late 1970s until today.

24

Since the late seventies, such efforts increased the working relationship of organizations on a national level. In 2003, a National Task Force to End Domestic and Sexual Violence Against Women was formed, comprising organizations primarily focused on addressing crimes of domestic violence, sexual assault, dating violence, and stalking.

The strength of the national alliance between Native and non-Native members, was tested during the 2012 national organizing campaign to reauthorize VAWA. The VAWA 2005 had expired on December 31, 2011, and Congress failed to reauthorize the Act until 500 days after it expired. Unlike prior reauthorizations, passage in 2013 came only after many months of difficult debate. The bipartisan VAWA bill, S. 47, passed the Senate on February 12, 2013, by a vote of 78 to 22. Every woman senator voted in support of the VAWA. The House passed the Senate version on February 28, 2013, by a vote of 286 to 138. Despite many difficult moments during the negotiation process over the legislation, the alliance maintained its unity and refused to support passage of a VAWA that did not include the tribal amendments restoring tribal jurisdiction over non-Indians and other amendments that are reviewed in the chapters that follow.

With VAWA 2013 reauthorized, all those concerned with safety and justice for Native women could now turn our attention toward implementation of this lifesaving legislation. The movement for safety of Native women must again roll up its sleeves to inform and educate all elected leaders of this nation and others to understand and support all provisions of the Act. The failure to reauthorize VAWA in 2011 was due in part to the staunch opposition of certain members of Congress to the tribal jurisdictional amendments. Much education is needed concerning violence against Native women, the sovereignty of Indian tribes, and how the VAWA tribal provisions can hold perpetrators of such crimes accountable for their violence. The future of VAWA will be shaped by a constant truth. The foundation of VAWA is the grassroots movement that created the Act. Specific to the tribal provisions it is the tribal women, advocates, and dedicated tribal leaders who breathe life into the VAWA as they have since its passage in 1994. Understanding the VAWA 2013 tribal amendments is an important task that lies before the movement—one that must be accomplished to make meaningful changes in the daily struggle of Native women for safety.

Native women have endured violence since colonization, and their blood continues to be shed due to the unjust and unacceptable loopholes in United States law. We are pleased that Congress has finally stepped up to address the unchecked violence against Native women by freeing the hands of Indian nations to protect Native women in their own communities from rapists and batterers.

—Juana Majel Dixon,
NCAI, First Vice President
Co-Chair NCAI Task Force on Violence Against Women
March 7, 2013

Chapter 1 Notes

[1] Juana Majel Dixon, June 18, 2003.

[2] Violence Against Women Act, Title IV of the Violent Crime Control and Law Enforcement Act of 1994 (Pub. L. 103-322) as amended by the Victims of Trafficking Protection Act of 2000 (Pub. L. 106-386), as amended by the Violence Against Women and Department of Justice Reauthorization Act of 2005 (H.R. 3402) as amended by Violence Against Women Reauthorization Act of 2013 (Pub. L. No. 113-114, 127 Stat. 54.).

[3] *Supra note* 2, Title IX. Safety for Indian Women.

[4] *Supra note* 2, Sec. 902 (2). *See also* inherent right of self-government codified in the Indian Reorganization Act of 1934, Ch. 576, 48 Stat. 984 (codified as amended at 25 U.S.C. §§ 461–479 (1994 & Supp. IV 1998)); Indian Civil Rights Act of 1968, Pub. L. No. 90–284, 82 Stat. 77 (codified as amended at 25 U.S.C. §§ 1301–1341 (1994 & Supp. IV 1998)); Indian Education Act of 1972, Pub. L. No. 992-318, 86 Stat. 873 (codified as amended in scattered sections of 7,12,16, and 20 U.S.C.); Indian Self-Determination and Education Assistance Act of 1975, Pub. L. No. 93-638, 88 Stat. 2206 (codified as amended in scattered sections of 5 U.S.C. and 25 U.S.C.); and American Indian Religious Freedom Act of 1978, Pub. L. No. 95-341, 92 Stat. 469 (codified as amended at 42 U.S.C. § 1996 (Supp. IV 1998)).

[5] Throughout this book, the term *Native* is used interchangeably with "American Indian" or "Alaska Native" when not specifically citing or paraphrasing other work. Native Hawaiians are not included in this reference because they have a distinct historical and contemporary legal relationship to the United States. *See generally Hawaii's Story by Hawaii's Queen* by Lili'uokalani, (Mutual Publishing, 1990) (1898) (International plea for justice by Queen Lili'uokalani for restoration of the Hawaiian throne and her nation to determine its own destiny); Apology Resolution of 1993, Pub. L. 103-150 (S.J. Res. 19) (apology to Native Hawaiians on behalf of the United States for the overthrow of the Kingdom of Hawaii); *Policy of the United States Regarding Its Relationship with Native Hawaiians; Hearing on S. 2899 Before the Subcommittee on Indian Affairs* (2000) (statement of Jacqueline Agtuca, Acting Director of Office of Tribal Justice, U.S. Dept. of Justice).

[6] "Beyond the Shelter Doors" Video, 2000, Jacqueline Agtuca.

[7] Chairman Hall as President of NCAI in 2003 strongly supported the establishment of the NCAI Task Force on Violence Against Women. He is an enrolled member of the Mandan, Hidatsa, and Arikara Nation. In November 2010, Chairman Hall was elected to an historic third term and is the longest-serving chairman of the tribe.

Chapter 2

Understanding VAWA in the Historical Context of the Colonization of Indian Nations[8]

A common question from both tribal and non-tribal people is, "Why is the rate of violence against American Indian women so much higher than violence committed against other women?" There are many answers to this question, and frequent responses include poverty, the remote nature of many reservations, and the lack of immediate access to law enforcement services, among other factors. The answer that links these responses together is the nature and circumstance of U.S. colonization of the indigenous peoples of North America. A history of forced assimilation and the current legal relationship of the United States to Indian tribes constitute the social fabric of contemporary violence perpetrated against Native women as a population. An ending point cannot exist without a beginning; thus ending violence against Native women requires an understanding of its historical beginning. The root of violence against Native women is not found in any single Congressional act, Supreme Court case, executive order, or federal policy but is revealed in the layers of federal laws and policies known as federal Indian law.[9]

The general public is typically unaware that three types of sovereigns exist in the United States: the federal government, tribal governments, and state governments.[10] As a result, the governmental responses available to assist Native women seeking safety from violence are defined not by a single body of law but frequently by a combination of tribal, federal, and state laws. Gaps in the law and lack of coordination in responding to such crimes for more than two hundred years have resulted in loopholes that allow perpetrators to walk free from legal consequences for crimes of violence. This body of bad laws is the result of the colonization and the

28

legal government-to-government relationship between Indian nations and the United States.

The inconsistent handling of violent crimes against Native women reaches far beyond the lack of training or failure of individuals to respond appropriately to such crimes. It is current federal law based on the historical relationship between the United States and Indian tribes as governments that shapes current legal authority over such crimes. This historic legal relationship also serves as the foundation for American cultural tolerance of violence against Native women. The current epidemic rates of violence against Native women are the contemporary mirror of the violence adopted by European nations[11] to achieve domination of Indian nations.[12]

"Let your women's sons be ours; our sons be yours. Let your women hear our words."[13] In 1781, a Cherokee woman named Nancy Ward spoke these good words while addressing the United States Treaty Commission at Holston. She believed that peace could only be sustained if the Cherokees and their enemies became one people bound by the ties of kinship. As a leader of the Cherokee Nation, she called upon the women of the United States, because in her worldview only the women could accomplish this goal. Theda Perdue writes, "The political power of Ward and other Cherokee women rested on their position as mothers in a matrilineal society that equated kinship and citizenship. In such a society, mothers—and by extension, women—enjoyed a great deal of honor and prestige, and references to motherhood evoked power rather than sentimentality."[14] Nancy Ward did not know that the women of the United States did not possess the authority to respond to her call for peace.

In 2005, 224 years after Nancy Ward's appeal to the women of the United States, Tex Hall, then President of the National Congress of American Indians (NCAI), stated: "Our women are abused at far greater rates than any other group of women in the United States. The rate of violent assault is so high because (the) lack of authority given to tribal police has created a system destined to fail our people and our women."[15]

The journey from 1781 to 2014 is that of the physical, cultural, and spiritual survival of Native women. In response to the imposition of foreign governments, Indian nations were forced to dismantle or modify their systems of governance. This disruption included a breakdown of customary law and tribal ways of life that safeguarded Native women from acts of physical and sexual abuse. The legalization and cultural acceptance of violence perpetrated against Native women as populations began with the conquest of Indian nations by colonial governments such as Spain, France,

Russia, and England.[16] An outstanding characteristic of conquest was the physical and cultural genocide of indigenous women of the Americas.

Under the dominion of each conquering nation, Native women became targets of the colonizer in the quest to conquer and assimilate Indian nations. Within the United States, the body of law and policy that governs the legal relationship between Indian nations and the United States is known as federal Indian law. It is within this legal context that Native women have witnessed a dramatic shift in their quality of life as a population. This legal relationship, established over more than two hundred years, separates Native women from other populations of women as illustrated in the following historical episodes.

As the aboriginal[17] people, Indian nations have always exercised the right of self-government, including authority over all persons committing acts of violence against women within their territorial lands. This authority of Indian nations over their members and land is known as inherent authority.[18] It is the natural and permanent authority that Indian nations have held over anyone coming within their territories for thousands of years. In an 1831 case arising between the Cherokee Indian Nation and the State of Georgia, Chief Justice John Marshall acknowledged, "The Cherokee Nation, then, is a distinct community, occupying its own territory, with boundaries accurately described, in which the laws of Georgia can have no force, and which the citizens of Georgia have no right to enter but with the assent of the Cherokees themselves or in conformity with the treaties and the acts of Congress."[19]

Independent of European nations, Indian nations make specific reference to the fact that they retain power to govern their land and the people who come within its boundaries. For example, among the Iroquois Confederacy, the Great Law addressed the Confederacy's jurisdiction:

Roots have spread out from the Tree of the Great Peace, one to the north, one to the east, one to the south, one to the west. The name of these roots is The Great White Roots and their nature is Peace and Strength. If any man or any nation outside the Five Nations shall obey the laws of the Great Peace and make known their disposition to the Lords of the Confederacy, they may trace the Roots to the Tree and if their minds are clean and they are obedient and promise to obey the wishes of the Confederate Council they shall be welcome to take shelter beneath the Tree of the Long Leaves.[20]

Women under the Great Law were granted rights and privileges that outlawed violent and abusive behavior, thereby creating a culture within the Five Nations that afforded fundamental safety to women.

Historical accounts of nations punishing offenders for abusing women exist on the opposite side of the continent as well. In the land now known as Alaska, Russian sailors were held accountable for abuse of Native women, as told in the story *Taa'ii' Ti'*:

> When the Russians landed, they fooled around with the Indian women during the night. There were lots of men in the big ship. The Chief named *Taa'ii' Ti'* told them not to bother the women, but they still did it, so he told them, "Don't ever do that again." He spoke very loudly. The Russian men he was talking to at that time were feeling his body muscles like this (gesturing) and said to him: "You have a weak body, why are you talking?" He was like a President himself so he was really mad when they told him that. He didn't say another word until everyone went to bed. The next morning, he reminded them not to do it again, but they still fooled around with the women, even the married women. The people in the village told him about it. The Russian men were sleeping at that time. They were sleeping in tents, and *Taa'ii' Ti'* got his cane and hit all of them. They all cried out in pain. While doing that he reminded them that they underestimated him and that his body was not weak. He only spared four men. They didn't like it, but what could they do about it. He ordered the rest of the men away to continue what they were being punished for. So the four men invited him to return with them since they knew he knew their own leader too. "Okay, yes," he said. So he went over with them. When they arrived (in Russia) they took him to the President there. *Taa'ii' Ti'* told him about the shipload of men that went over to Alaska and how he killed them all that one morning.[21]

Historically, violence against Native women was rare because such behavior was inconsistent with the role of women within the worldview of Indian nations. When such behavior occurred, the nation appropriately addressed the offender's action. For example, among the Tlingit people, perpetrators of domestic violence crimes were tied to stakes during low tide and justice was left to greater powers. If the perpetrator survived, then he survived. If not, then he did not. This punishment was well known for such crimes.[22] The wishes and roles of the aggrieved woman were central to the response from the community. Violence was considered inappropriate behavior, and the well-being of the woman was central to restoring the balance of the community. Thus, the family, the clan, as well as spiritual and tribal leaders held essential roles in the process of holding offenders accountable for their actions.

Offenders were often removed from the tribe through banishment or execution, or whipped or publicly humiliated within the specific practice of the tribe. The Payne Papers contain the following report of the death of a Cherokee Chief:

> Doublehead had beaten his wife cruelly when she was with child, and the poor woman died in consequence. The revenge against the murder now became, in the Indian's conscience, imperative. The wife of Doublehead was the sister of the wife of (James) Vann. Vann's wife desired with her own hand to obtain atonement for her sister's death. Vann acquiesced; and he and a large party of friends set away with his wife upon the mission of blood. [23]

The high standard of accountability for acts of violence against women while common to Indian tribes was specific to each tribe in terms of consequences. Based on the beliefs and circumstances of the community, an abuser would be held accountable. Rose Borkowski, Yup'ik Eskimo, describes the accountability of abusers in her village during the fifties as direct and with severe consequences:

> The men talk to that person, and the object was to retrain the man how to treat his wife, to show respect. If they were repeat abusers, if they didn't learn their lesson, then they'd be told to pack up, like, extra clothing, hunting gear, and food and told to go out into the wilderness, the tundra, and survive the experience of living alone. When the men check him, he was allowed to come back into the village and allowed to go back to his wife, instead of being punished like they are taking into jail today, fined, and all that. They were no actual council members, but everybody, all the men, were involved in this problem. If the man continued to be abusive he was asked to go to another village not to have contact with his wife and children.[24]

The safety of women was and continues to be directly linked to the inherent authority of Indian nations to utilize the power of government to

32

protect their well-being. However, things changed for Native women after the arrival of Europeans. It became more difficult for Indian nations to protect their women with restrictions of tribal sovereignty imposed by the United States. Colonization and the destruction and dismantling of the governments of Indian nations were directly connected to the taking of Indian lands and resources.

Taking of Lands

Attacks on Native culture began with land acquisition. The legal fiction for creating a basis for land title in North America was the Doctrine of Discovery. Under this doctrine, the sovereign discoverer could occupy land already occupied by infidels to extend Christian sovereignty over the land and the indigenous people who resided there.[25]

The initial dispute between foreign conquerors and Indian nations over land has continued over time. In 1823, the Supreme Court incorporated into U.S. law the Doctrine of Discovery. Chief Justice John Marshall wrote in *Johnson v. McIntosh*, "As the United States marched across the continent, it was creating an empire by wars of foreign conquest just as England and France were doing in India and Africa. In every case, the goal was identical: land." The taking of tribal lands through these wars altered the relationship of Indian nations, and specifically Native women, to their homelands.

Through treaties, Indian nations exchanged lands and resources for peace and recognition of their sovereignty. The interpretation of language contained in such treaties was frequently not according to the life ways of Indian nations but that of the United States. One example is the claim of Sally Ladiga and her heirs to land under the Treaty of New Echota, enacted in 1832:

> Under the treaty, Indian heads of families were to be allotted 320 acres of land to live on and cultivate. Local federally appointed "locating agents" decided who was an Indian and who was the head of a family and allotted heads of families the land on which they resided and had made improvements. When Ladiga was enrolled, she had a cabin and a cultivated field on her land, had raised a family of several children, but had no husband of record. The only people recorded living with her were another woman, Sarah Letter, and a boy named Ar-chee-chee. In spite of evidence that Ladiga bought clothes for Ar-chee-chee, as well as conflicting

evidence that he was Ladiga's orphaned grandson, the locating agent found that Ladiga was not the head of a family and was not entitled to a half section of the land . . . Despite all Sally Ladiga's efforts to continue living upon her land, a soldier forcibly removed her from it. A white man named Smith entered her land and took over her cabin and field. Armed troops forced Ladiga to immigrate to Indian territory in Arkansas.[26]

In 1844, the U.S. Supreme Court held that Sally Ladiga was indeed the head of a family.[27] "We cannot seriously discuss the question, whether a grandmother and her grandchildren compose a family, in the meaning of that word in the treaty, it must shock the common sense of all mankind to even doubt it."[28] Although years later, the Supreme Court's recognized Sally Ladiga as "a head of family," it did not benefit her or her heirs. Sally Ladiga apparently died on the Trail of Tears and her grandchildren could not legally prove that she was their ancestor.

Native women also suffered the loss of their communally held tribal homelands through the General Allotment Act (passed by Congress), which conveyed personal ownership of land to individual Indians.[29] Prior to the Allotment Act, most Indian nations held land collectively. It is estimated that Indian nations lost 90 million acres of land due to the Act, displacing hundreds of Native women and families. The Act was interpreted inconsistently in different regions of the United States. In some regions, women could not receive allotments as heads of household. As a result, many tribal women became landless. Additionally, Native women who did receive individual allotments frequently lost land to non-Indian men. In many cases, non-Indian men married Native women to gain access to land and resources.[30] The large number of murdered women of the Osage Nation of Oklahoma finally sparked a federal investigation.[31] While the Allotment Act was later abolished, it had a devastating impact upon Indian nations, especially upon the lives of Native women. Many Native women went from holding a strong role in a communal land setting to being landless.

Federal Indian Policy and the Safety of Native Women

Historically, federal policy toward Indian nations has eroded the protections and status of Native women within their respective nations and within the United States. Federal policies served to guide the actions of federal departments or agencies and were an additional legal dimension that supported the cultural acceptance of violence committed against Native women. Certain policies during the Indian Wars, the Boarding School Era, the Adoption Era, and period of forced sterilization highlight the devastating impact such federal policies had upon the lives of Native women.

During the Indian Wars, Native women and their children were targeted. Phrases such as "kill and scalp all, big and little" and "nits make lice" became a rallying cry for the troops (i.e., since Indians were "lice," their children were "nits"; the only way to get rid of lice was to kill the nits as well). This policy of extermination legalized the killing of Native women. To avoid being killed or having children murdered, Indian women were forced to assimilate. Assimilation for Native women meant relinquishing honored, multifaceted roles within their nations and adopting the role of non-Indian women within the United States. Typically, Native women were instructed on domestic tasks of servants.

The Boarding School Era, from the 1880s to the 1950s, followed by the Adoption Era, from the 1950s to the 1970s, removed, many times forcibly, the children of Native women in order to further the federal policy of assimilation. This policy was clearly a violation of the concept of a "mother's right." It also negatively impacted the customs and traditions of many Indian nations for the mother and the maternal relatives to have the cultural responsibility for raising children. Therefore, these policies took away from tribal women and their nations the role of women to raise and pass on cultural traditions to their children.

The intent of these two eras is captured in the following statement of the 1886 Commissioner of Indian Affairs:

> It is admitted by most people that the adult savage is not susceptible to the influence of civilization, and we must therefore turn to his children, that they might be taught to abandon the pathway of barbarism and walk with a sure step along the pleasant highway of Christian civilization . . . They must be withdrawn, in tender years, entirely from the camp and taught to eat, to sleep, to dress, to play, to work, to think after the manner of the white man.[32]

There was a specific intent to disrupt the family bond in order to assimilate Indian children. The cultural genocide committed through the forced removal of Native children is well documented as having lifelong detrimental effects on Indian families. One girl later wrote, "I cried aloud, shaking my head all the while until I felt the cold blades of the scissors against my neck, and heard them gnaw off one of my thick braids. Then I lost my spirit."[33] The consequences for resisting the removal of their children to government boarding school were severe for parents.[34] Further, the physical and sexual violence committed against girls by employees of the government schools further normalized violence committed against Native women.[35]

Another era highlighting the negative impact of federal policy upon Native women implemented in healthcare facilities and primarily by the Indian Health Service was a policy of eugenics. Native women were the subjects of a policy described as "forced sterilization"[36] by the Department of Health and Human Services, Indian Health Service, and other healthcare facilities:

> My husband beat me bad that day. After he left I crawled outside to the street and someone called an ambulance. When I woke up I was in the hospital. I was covered in bruises and my body ached. My stomach had a patch over it covering a wound. I asked the nurse, "Did my husband do this?" She answered, "No, you had a hysterectomy." I didn't know what the word even meant. When she explained I just cried.[37]

Congress investigated the sterilization of Native women at Indian Health Service facilities and contract facilities. In 1976, the Comptroller General released a summary report.[38] The investigation, while limited to four areas of the United States for a period of three years, revealed that Native women, without their informed consent, were being sterilized. The report states:

> Indian Health Service records show that 3,406 sterilization procedures were performed on female Indians in the Aberdeen, Albuquerque, Oklahoma City, and Phoenix areas during fiscal years 1973–1976. Data for fiscal year 1976 is for a 120-month period ending June 30, 1976. Of the 3,406 procedures performed, 3,001 involved women of child-bearing age (ages 15 to 44), and 1,024 were performed at Indian Health Service contract facilities. On April 18, 1974, the U.S. District Court for the District of Columbia issued regulations to address the sterilization of persons by the Indian Health Service.

In summary, the trauma Native peoples have experienced resulting from colonization is linked to current epidemic levels of violence experienced by Native women. Furthermore, the impact of U.S. federal law and policy is clearly the foundation for social acceptance of a system that offers one level of protection for Native women and another for all other women. The depth of the erosion of respect for and physical safety of Native women resulting from U.S. federal polices is societal and intergenerational. The fact that Native women are victimized at rates of more than double that of any other population of women in the United States must be understood in this historical context. Perhaps, the most significant lesson gained in review of the negative impact that federal law and policy has had upon Native women is the need to amend current laws and policies that operate to diminish the legal authority of Indian nations to protect their women.

Chapter 2 Notes

[8] This chapter draws from an earlier article by the author published in 2008: Jacqueline Agtuca, "Beloved Women: Life Givers, Caretakers, Teachers of Future Generations," in *Sharing Our Stories of Survival, Native Women Surviving Violence* (2008) pp. 3–26.

[9] Federal Indian law refers to codes, cases, and executive orders of the United States and not the tribal law of specific Indian nations.

[10] Hon. Sandra Day O'Connor, *Lessons from the Third Sovereign: Indian Tribal Courts*, Tribal Court Record, National Indian Justice Center, Vol. 9, No. 1, 1996.

[11] Russia, France, England, and Spain negotiated with and followed similar patterns of violence through warfare against Indian nations and Native women. See Herman J. Viola, *Diplomats in Buckskins History of Indian Delegations in Washington City* (Rivilo Books, 1995, originally published by the Smithsonian Institution Press, 1981).

[12] David E. Stannard, *American Holocaust: the Conquest of the New World* (Oxford University Press 1992).

[13] Nathaniel Green Papers (Library of Congress), quoted in Samuel Cole Williams, *Tennessee During the Revolutionary War*, 201 (University of Tennessee Press, 1974).

[14] Theda Perdue, *Cherokee Women, Gender and Cultural Change* 1700–1835, 101 (University of Nebraska Press, 1998).

[15] Tex Red Tipped Arrow Hall, *President's Report*, 2005 Executive Council Winter Session (Feb. 28, 2005).

[16] *See generally* Virginia M. Bouvier, *Women and Conquest of California, 1542–1840* (University of Arizona Press); Karen Anderson, *Chain Her By One Foot: The Subjugation of Native Women in Seventeenth-Century New France* (Routledge 1991); Ann Fienup-Riordan, *Boundaries and Passages, Rule and Ritual in Yup'ik Eskimo Oral Tradition* (University of Oklahoma Press, 1994).

[17] *ab origine* meaning "from the beginning"

[18] *United States v. Wheeler*, 435 U.S. 313 (1978). Here, it is evident from the treaties between the Navajo Tribe and the United States and from the various statutes establishing federal criminal jurisdiction over crimes involving Indians, that the Navajo Tribe has never given up its sovereign power to punish tribal offenders, nor has that power implicitly been lost by virtue of the Indian's dependent status; thus, tribal exercise of that power is presently the continued exercise of retained tribal sovereignty (pp. 323–326). Respondent, a member of the Navajo Tribe, pleaded guilty in tribal court to a charge of contributing to the delinquency of a minor and was sentenced. Subsequently, he was indicted by a federal grand jury for statutory rape of a 15-year-old girl arising out of the same incident.

[19] *Cherokee Nation v. Georgia*, 30 U.S. (5 Pet.) 1 (1831).

[20] The Constitution of the Iroquois Nations, The Great Binding Law, Gayanashagowa, 2, University of Oklahoma Law Center. Available at www.law.ou.edu/iroquois.html.

[21] Johnny Frank, Athabascan Elder, as cited in Carrie E. Garrow and Sarah Deer, *Tribal Criminal Law and Procedure* (AltaMira Press, 2004).

[22] Telephone interview with Tammy Young, member, Sitka Tribe of Alaska (Aug. 1999) and Co-Director of the Alaska Native Women's Coalition.

[23] As cited by Theda Perdue, *Cherokee Women, Gender and Cultural Change*, 1700–1835 (University of Nebraska Press, 1998).

[24] Rose Borkowski, video interview, Native Village of Emmonak, 2004, transcript on file with the author.

[25] Roe Bubar and Pamela Jumper Thurman, "Violence Against Native Women," *Social Justice*, Vol. 31, No. 4, 73 (2004).

[26] Bethany Ruth Berger, *After Pocahontas: Indian Women and the Law*, 1830– 1934, 21, *American Indian Law Review*, Vol. 1, No. 7 (1997).

[27] Ladiga II, 43 U.S. (2 How.) at 583.

[28] *Id.*

[29] Act of February 8, 1887, 24 Stat. 388.

[30] *Moore v. United States*, 150 U.S. 57 (1893). Palmer's land was rented from an Indian. This land was also claimed by a full-blooded Choctaw woman named Lizzie Lishtubbi. Four days before the murder, defendant Moore married this woman. He had previously boasted that he was going to marry the woman and get the land, "that she was old and would not live long, and he would get a good stake." One of the witnesses told him that he would have trouble over it, as Charles Palmer was about the gamiest man in the territory. He replied: "I am some that way myself." As he started to leave, he said: "I may not get to marry the widow, and if I do not, if you give me away, I will kill you."

[31] Dennis McAuliffe, *Bloodland: A Family Story of Oil, Greed and Murder on the Osage Reservation* (Council Oak Books, 1999). Lawrence J. Hogan, *The Osage Indian Murders: The True Story of a 21-Murder Plot to Inherit the Headrights of Wealthy Osage Tribe Members* (AMLEX, Inc., 1988)

[32] Monroe E. Price, *Law and the American Indian Contemporary Legal Education Series* (1973), quoted in Lila J. George, "Why the Need for the Indian Child Welfare Act?," *Journal of Multicultural Social Work*, Vol. 5, No. 166 (1997).

[33] "School Days of an Indian Girl," *Atlantic Monthly*, Vol. 85, Issue 508 (1900).

[34] Nineteen Hopi fathers were arrested and imprisoned for over a year at Alcatraz for failing to enroll their children in a government boarding school with deplorable conditions. Wendy Holliday, *Hopi History: The Story of the Alcatraz Prisoners*. Available at http://www.nps.gov/alca/historyculture/hopi-prisoners-on-the-rock.htm.

[35] U.S. Congress, Senate, Committee on Indian Affairs, Survey of the Conditions of the Indians in the United States, Hearings before a Subcommittee of the Committee on Indian Affairs, Senate, on SR 79, 70th Cong., 2nd session, 1929, 428–429, 1021–1023, and 2833–2835.

[36] *See generally* Michael Sullivan DeFine, *A History of Governmentally Coerced Sterilization: The Plight of the Native American Wom*an, University of Maine School of Law (1997). Available at http://www.whale.to/b/define.html. Charles R. England, *A Look at the Indian Health Service Policy of Sterilization*, 1972–1976, at 1. Available at www.dickshovel.com/IHSSterPol.html.

[37] Testimony (identity withheld at the request of the presenter) Alaska Native Women's Coalition Conference, Anchorage, Alaska, 2003.

[38] Comptroller General of the United States, B-164031(5), Nov. 23, 1976. The regulations specified; "(1) continued a July 1973 moratorium on sterilizing persons who were under 21 years of age or mentally incompetent, (2) specified the informed consent procedure for persons legally capable of consenting to sterilization, and (3) omitted the requirement that individuals seeking sterilization be orally informed at the outset that no Pedersi benefits can be withdrawn because of failure to accept sterilization."

Chapter 3

Legal Barriers to the Safety of Native Women

Federal Indian law is often analogized to the swinging of the pendulum. The original passage of VAWA in 1994, and subsequent reauthorizations in 2000, 2005, and 2013 clearly reflect a positive swing and, hopefully, a continuing trend in federal policy. For all who understand this reality, the successes of VAWA over two decades represent a challenge to continue to move forward until Native women and all women can live free of violence. Through education and increased awareness of the origins of violence against Native women, tribal nations can create a pathway toward its eventual elimination. Understanding the connection of contemporary violence to the legal barriers preventing the safety of Native women is a social process important to reforming justice systems. While many barriers exist on federal and state levels, some are more significant than others. If the violence committed against Native women is likened to a house, these barriers serve as the corner posts of the house.

"The jurisdictional limitations that the U.S. law places on Indian nations have created an unworkable and discriminatory race-based system for administering justice in Native communities. This system denies Native people, particularly Native women, their right to life, security, equal treatment under the law, and access to meaningful and effective judicial remedies."[39]

In exchange for lands and resources, the United States guaranteed the protection of the sovereignty of Indian nations. The language of treaties signed by the United States and Indian nations indicates that lands were set aside for the exclusive use of Indian nations.[40] The U.S. Supreme Court has also affirmed that tribes retain the inherent right of self-government unless explicitly removed by Congress.[41] Specifically, the Court has stated that tribal government authority includes "the power to punish tribal offenders . . . to regulate domestic relations among members."[42] In addition, the Court added that tribes retained inherent sovereign power, even on fee lands, to regulate conduct of non-Indians that threatens or directly affects "the health or welfare of the tribe."[43] All of this envelops the federal trust responsibility of the United States, which Congress has defined to include "the protection of the sovereignty of each tribal government."[44]

The federal trust responsibility assures tribes that the United States will defend the right of Indian nations to self-government. The United States has a trust responsibility to promote the welfare of Indian tribes, which includes a duty to assist tribes in making their reservations livable homes.[45] Within this broad context lies the responsibility of the United States to assist Indian nations in safeguarding the safety and well-being of Native women from violence. In 2005, Congress reauthorized the VAWA to include a specific title to address violence against Native women, finding that "the unique legal relationship of the United States to Indian tribes creates a federal trust responsibility to assist tribal governments in safeguarding the lives of Indian women."[46]

Contrary to the federal trust responsibility, both Congress and the Supreme Court have over time restricted the jurisdictional authority of Indian nations, resulting in the erosion of the legal ability of tribal governments to fully protect its citizens. The impact of this steady erosion of tribal sovereignty upon the safety of women citizens has resulted in less legal protection for Native women than for other women in the United States. Since 1994, Congress has, with the reauthorization of each VAWA, clarified and acknowledged the inherent sovereign authority of Indian tribes to respond to and protect Native women from violent crimes. While the pattern is a positive shift toward the recognition of sovereignty and authority of Indian tribes to assist Native women fleeing violence, much work remains to unravel outstanding, far-reaching legal barriers ingrained in federal Indian law. The review of the following Congressional acts, Supreme Court case, and treaty responsibilities highlights significant current legal barriers the United States imposed upon the authority of Indian nations to respond to violence against Native women. The positive reform patterns reflected in the Congressional amendments to certain components of federal Indian law over the last 20 years is also discussed.

The first erosion of tribal sovereignty is reflected in the passage of the Major Crimes Act in 1885, wherein the U.S. government through an act of Congress assumed concurrent jurisdiction over serious crimes[47] committed by an Indian in Indian country. This Act specifically included crimes of violence that are often found to form a pattern of behavior typical of domestic violence perpetrators: the crimes of murder, kidnapping, maiming, assault with intent to commit murder, assault with a dangerous weapon, assault resulting in serious bodily injury, and, later, sexual abuse.[48] This intrusion was devastating because these are crimes that relate to acts of violence commonly committed against women. Although Indian tribes had concurrent misdemeanor authority over such crimes, the Act severely undermined tribal authority.[49]

The extension of federal jurisdiction over crimes enumerated under the Major Crimes Act eroded the traditional response of tribal governments to such crimes by sending the incorrect message that Indian nations could not properly handle such cases. While federal jurisdiction was concurrent with that of an Indian tribe, a myth emerged following passage of the Act that the federal government could and would prosecute such crimes. Since 1885, the harsh reality is that felony level crimes against Native women are typically not prosecuted by the United States. Unfortunately, this lack of federal prosecution has created the public perception that such crimes are not considered to be serious crimes.

In addition, the passage of the Major Crimes Act created a myth that criminal jurisdiction of Indian tribes over such crimes was removed and that Indian tribes did not have authority to prosecute crimes included under the Major Crimes Act. The lack of tribal criminal justice response to rape or sexual assault of Native women was often based on the mistaken belief that Indian tribes did not have authority over crimes such as sexual assault. Since passage of VAWA in 1994, this inaccuracy has steadily decreased, particularly as grants under VAWA programs have been awarded to Indian tribes to enhance their response to sexual assault. Also, Indian tribes are increasingly actively engaging in enacting codes to address sexual assault, forming sexual assault response teams, and developing advocacy services for rape victims. Statements issued by Attorney Generals Janet Reno and Eric Holder in support of Indian tribes exercising their concurrent authority over these crimes have assisted in this clarification.

Indian Civil Rights Act

The second significant erosion of tribal sovereignty can be found in the 1968 Indian Civil Rights Act provision that limits the sentencing authority of tribal courts to "in no event impose for conviction of any one offense any penalty or punishment greater than imprisonment for a term of one year and a fine of $5,000, or both." This limitation severely restricts the ability of tribal governments to appropriately respond to serious crimes of violence against Native women, including sexual assault and domestic abuse.[50] The limitations also reinforced the myth that offenders of such crimes will not incur significant legal consequence or criminal penalties.

In 2010, Congress responded to the negative impact of this restriction on the ability of tribal courts to appropriately respond to crimes of domestic and sexual violence against Native women by amending the Indian Civil Rights Act. Responding to growing public opinion on the injustice of a one-year maximum sentence for a crime such as rape, Congress increased the sentencing authority of tribal courts. Indian tribes meeting the requirements established under the Tribal Law and Order Act of 2010 (TLOA)[51] now have the authority to sentence a defendant per offense to three years and a fine of $15,000, or both. While this amendment increases the sentencing authority to a more appropriate level, it does not provide tribal courts the same sentencing authority as states or federal courts for crimes such as rape.

Supreme Court Ruling in Oliphant v. Suquamish

The third act of erosion occurred with the 1978 U.S. Supreme Court case of *Oliphant v. Suquamish* in which the Court ruled that Indian nations lacked authority to prosecute crimes committed by non-Indians.[52] This landmark shift in criminal jurisdiction by the Court altered the ability of Indian nations to hold accountable non-Indian offenders committing violent acts. Indian tribes, while continuing to exercise civil jurisdiction over these offenders, also encounter the public perception that non-Indians can commit such crimes without significant consequences. The *Oliphant* decision created a jurisdictional loophole for non-Indian perpetrators of violence against Native women living on tribal lands, as tribal governments could no longer hold these abusers criminally accountable. This U.S. Supreme Court–created loophole allowed non-Indians to commit heinous acts of physical and sexual abuse without fear of any legal consequence from tribal governments.

Congress has acted to partially close this legal loophole by restoring limited criminal jurisdiction to participating Indian tribes under the VAWA 2013[53] amendment to the Indian Civil Rights Act. Under the 2013 tribal amendment to VAWA, Indian tribes can arrest and prosecute non-Indian offenders committing a limited set of crimes: domestic violence, dating violence, and protection order violations. The specific requirements for an Indian tribe to implement special domestic violence criminal jurisdiction are discussed in the following chapter.

Public Law 83-280 (PL 280)

In 1953, Congress increased the jurisdictional complexity confronting Indian nations by enacting Public Law 83-280 (PL 280).[54] As an extension of the federal policy to "terminate" Indian tribes, Congress withdrew federal criminal jurisdiction on reservations in six states[55] and authorized those states to assume criminal jurisdiction on Indian lands[56] and permitted all other states to acquire it at their option. Under PL 280 state jurisdiction, federal responsibility for the prosecution of serious crimes, such as sexual assault, under the Major Crimes Act[57] was transferred to state law enforcement agencies. While PL 280 did not alter the civil or criminal jurisdictional authority of tribal governments, tribes located in PL 280 jurisdictions were denied federal funds to support the development of tribal justice systems.[58] Furthermore, the transfer of federal responsibility to the state governments to provide law enforcement services to Indian nations was not accompanied with the allocation of any funds to support such services. Today, many tribes located in PL 280 states do not have emergency or other law enforcement services that should be provided by states and do not receive funding from the federal government to develop such services themselves. Native women living within PL 280 states frequently report that crimes of physical or sexual assault are typically not addressed. The consequences of PL 280 are far-reaching and tragic.[59]

Congress, recognizing the pattern of failed responses to cases of domestic and sexual violence on PL 280 tribal lands, created a legal path under the TLOA of 2010[60] for Indian tribes to petition the federal government to reassume federal criminal jurisdiction. On March 15, 2013, the Department of Justice announced that it had granted the first resumption request and would accept concurrent jurisdiction with the White Earth Indian Nation over its reservation in Minnesota.

Treaty Responsibility

> If bad men among the whites, or among other people subject to the authority of the United States, shall commit any wrong upon the person or property of the Indians, the United States will, upon proof made to the agent, and forwarded to the Commissioner of Indian Affairs at Washington city, proceed at once to cause the offender to be arrested and punished according to the laws of the United States, and also reimburse the injured person for the loss sustained.

—Bad Men Treaty Clause, 1868

In addition to these Congressional and Supreme Court actions, the ability of Indian nations to protect women citizens was also eroded through the United States' failure to uphold its obligations under treaties signed with over 100 Indian nations. Indian nations that entered into treaties with the United States did so on a nation-to-nation basis.[61] This government-to-government relationship recognized the inherent sovereign authority of Indian nations over their lands and peoples. In this context, Indian nations held full authority to protect women citizenry from foreign individuals who choose to enter their lands and commit acts of violence against women.

The first lawsuit specifically filed on behalf of a Native woman for sexual assault under the Bad Men Treaty Clause was not until 2006. Lavetta Elk filed her suit against the United States for sexual molestation by a white Army recruiter. She successfully sued the United States based on a violation of the Bad Men clause of the 1868 Fort Laramie Treaty. Based on the violation of the treaty clause, a federal court awarded her nearly $600,000 for her pain and suffering.

In 2002, Lavetta Elk was 19 years old and living on the Pine Ridge Indian Reservation in Wounded Knee. U.S. Army Sergeant Joseph P. Kopf recruited Ms. Elk to join the Army. Following an evaluation by the U.S. Army in Sioux Falls, to which Kopf drove Ms. Elk, she was informed that she was admitted into the U.S. Army. Following these initial interactions, Kopf initiated direct contact with Ms. Elk on a number of occasions. Ms. Elk moved to Kansas City in August 2002 to attend school. Kopf reportedly telephoned and emailed her there, approximately three times per day. When Ms. Elk returned to the Pine Ridge Indian Reservation, Kopf made repeated excuses to visit and call her at home. On January 7, 2003, Sergeant Kopf made an unannounced visit to her home, and told her father, Emerson Elk, that she needed to travel to Sioux Falls to resubmit her height and weight evaluation, claiming that the original evaluation had been lost. As she had before, Ms. Elk accompanied the Sergeant in his car to go to the supposed evaluation. She later testified that he drove her to an isolated area and sexually assaulted her. She reported the incident to the Bureau of Indian Affairs police, the Oglala Nation tribal police, and eventually the Army recruiting station where Sergeant Kopf was stationed.

The case of Lavetta Elk was the first to raise the specific responsibility of the United States for crimes of sexual violence against a Native woman and provides a larger context for this treaty clause. "The broader view of the Bad Men clause finds support in the history of the 1868 Fort Laramie Treaty. The Treaty of 1868 "was concluded at the culmination of the Powder River War of 1866–1867, a series of military engagements in which the Sioux tribes, led by their great chief, Red Cloud, fought to protect the integrity of earlier-recognized treaty lands from the incursion of white settlers."[62] In 1867, various tribal leaders spoke to Congress about the mistreatment of their people by white men. Their testimony documented the mistreatment of the women in their nations, who were killed, mutilated, attacked, and coerced into prostitution and other sexual relationships with U.S. soldiers. This testimony was well-documented in *Conditions of the Indian Tribes: Report of the Joint Special Committee Appointed Under Joint Resolution of March 3, 1865*, S. Rep. 39-156 (1867), commonly known as the Doolittle Commission Report.[63] The sexual offenses committed by whites were particularly pernicious as they led to the spread of syphilis, which ravaged the women and men of the tribes, causing many deaths.[64] Finding that a "large majority of cases [of] Indian Wars are to be traced to the aggressions of lawless white men," the report urged that various steps be taken "to preserve amity" and "save the government from unnecessary and expensive Indian Wars."[65]

The Choctaw and Chickasaw Nations also safeguarded authority to protect women citizens by including language providing for jurisdiction over non-Indian persons choosing to reside within the boundaries of the nation:

Every white person who, having married a Choctaw or Chickasaw, resides in the said Choctaw or Chickasaw Nation, or who has been adopted by the legislative authorities, is to be deemed a member of said nation, and shall be subject to the laws of the Choctaw and Chickasaw Nations according to his domicile, and to prosecution and trial before their tribunals, and to punishment according to their laws in all respects as though he was a native Choctaw or Chickasaw.[66]

In earlier treaties, Indian nations also provided protections for women citizenry by including clauses specific to women.[67] These specific sections reflect concern for the safety of Native women and the need to establish clauses for their protection. According to these treaties entered into by the United States with various Indian nations, Native women could rely on their governments for protection from individual acts of abuse by their husbands and other men threatening their safety. It is unfortunate that the first case under the Bad Men clause did not occur until 2006, but the pattern of reform as a result of a national movement for the safety of Native women is developing in a positive direction.

Chapter 3 Notes

[39] Terri Henry, Councilwoman, Eastern Band of Cherokee Indians, before the United Nations, Department of Economic and Social Affairs, Secretariat of the Permanent Forum on Indigenous Issues, January 2012.

[40] In 1868, the Second Treaty of Fort Laramie established the Crow Reservation and provided that the reservation "shall be . . . set apart for the absolute and undisturbed use and occupation" of the tribe, and that no non-Indians except government agents "shall ever be permitted to pass over, settle upon, or reside in the reservation." The United States now solemnly agrees that no persons, except those herein designated and authorized to do so, and except such officers, agents, and employees of the government as may be authorized to enter upon Indian reservations in discharge of duties enjoined by law, "shall ever be permitted to pass over, settle upon, or reside in the territory described in this article for the use of said Indians . . . ." (450 U.S. 544, 554). Second Treaty of Fort Laramie, May 7, 1868, Article, II, 15 Stat. 650. Similarly the Article II of the Treaty of Medicine Creek, 10 Stat. 1132 provided that the Puyallup Reservation was to be "set apart, and, so far as necessary, surveyed, and marked out for their exclusive use" and that no "white man [was to] be permitted to reside upon the same without permission of the tribe and the superintendent or agent."

[41] *United States v. Wheeler*, 435 U.S. 313 (1978). *See also* President Bush, Executive Memorandum to Executive Departments and Agencies signed Sept. 23, 2004; President Clinton, Executive Order 13175, Consultation and Coordination with Indian Tribal Governments, Nov. 6, 2000.

[42] *Montana v. United States*, 450 U.S. at 564 (1981).

[43] 450 U.S. at 565–66.

[44] 25 U.S.C. 3601.

[45] *See Montana v. United States*, 450 U.S. 544, 56 & no. 15 (1980).

[46] Title IX, Section 2 of the Violence Against Women and Department of Justice Reauthorization Act of 2005, Public Law 109-162, as amended by Public Law 109-271.

[47] Seven crimes were originally covered, but the list has been expanded to the present 14 by a series of amendments.

[48] Major Crimes Act, 18 U.S.C.A. 1153 (1885).

[49] *United States v. Lara*, 541 U.S. 193 (2004). Because the tribe acted in its capacity as a sovereign authority, the Double Jeopardy Clause does not prohibit the federal government from proceeding with the present prosecution for a discrete federal offense (pp. 4–16). Domestic violence case during which a federal officer was assaulted.

[50] Indian Civil Rights Act, 25 U.S.C. 1302(7) (1968).

[51] Tribal Law and Order Act of 2010, Pub. L. No. 111-211, Title II, 124 Stat. 2261 (codified as amended in scattered sections of the U.S. Code).

[52] *Oliphant v. Suquamish Indian Tribe*, 435 U.S. 191 (1978).

[53] Violence Against Women Reauthorization Act of 2013, Pub. L. No 113-4, §204(d).

[54] Public Law 83-280, 67 Stat. 588 (1953).

[55] The six named states, known as the "mandatory states," are: California, Minnesota (except Red Lake Reservation), Nebraska, Oregon (except the Warm Springs Reservation), Wisconsin, and, as added in 1958, Alaska (except the Annette Islands with regard to the Metlakatla Indians).

[56] PL 280 also conferred civil jurisdiction on the mandatory states, 28 U.S.C.A. 1360 (a), that is confined to adjudicatory jurisdiction only. *Bryan v. Itasca County*, 426 U.S. 373 (1976).

[57] PL 280 provided that the General Crimes Act (18 U.S.C.A. 1152) and the Major Crimes Act (18 U.S.C.A. 1153) no longer applied to areas covered by PL 280 in the mandatory states. 18 U.S.C.A. 1162.

[58] *See generally* C. Goldberg-Ambrose and D. Champagne, *A Second Century of Dishonor: Federal Inequities and California Tribes*, Report to the Advisory Council on California Indian Policy, 47–59 (1996).

[59] *See generally* Carole Goldberg-Ambrose, *Planting Tail Feathers: Tribal Survival and Public Law 280* (American Indian Studies Center, 1997).

[60] Tribal Law and Order Act §234(a)(3).

[61] Not all Indian nations entered into a treaty with the United States. Further, the United States Congress failed to ratify hundreds of treaties negotiated with Indian nations. Vine Deloria Jr. and David E. Wilkins, *Tribes, Treaties, and Constitutional Tribulations* (University of Texas Press, 1999).

[62] *United States v. Sioux Nation of Indians*, 448 U.S. 371, 374 (1980).

[63] See id. at App. 29, 42, 51, 53, 56-57, 60-75, 96-97, 205, 234, 249, 251-255, 259-263, 326, 332, 356, 360, 371, 386, 407-409, 417-418, 466-470, 499 (describing the mistreatment of Indian women); id. at App. 371, 386, 465, 469-470 (describing the coercion of Indian women into sex, often in exchange for food for starving children).

[64] See id. at 5, App. 428, 480.

[65] See id. at 5, 9. Opinion of Judge Allegra, *Elk v. United States*.

[66] Article 38 of the treaty with the Choctaws and Chickasaws, of April 28, 1866 (14 Stat. 779).

[67] Article 6, Republic of Mexico Treaty with the Navajo Chieftains, July 15, 1839 (Treaty consisted of seven articles) stated: "In case any Navajo Indian woman succeeds in escaping by fleeing from the house of her master, on arrival of the said woman in her own land, when it is verified, that she remain free and without any obligation of the nation to give anything for her ransom." Translation from Jenkins and Minge, pp. 51–52.

Chapter 4

Understanding VAWA and
Title IX. Safety for Indian Women

> The unique legal relationship of the United States to Indian tribes
> creates a federal trust responsibility to assist tribal governments in
> safeguarding the lives of Indian women.[68]

Overview of VAWA 1994, 2000, 2005, 2013

In 1994, the United States Congress passed the Violence Against
Women Act (VAWA),[69] marking the federal government's recognition of
the extent and seriousness of violence against women. VAWA was
reauthorized in 2000 [70], 2005 [71], and 2013 [72]. The enactment and
reauthorizations in 2000 and 2005 were by unanimous consent of the
House and Senate. Certain Republican members opposed special tribal
jurisdiction during the reauthorization of VAWA in 2012, which resulted in
the expiration of the Act. On February 28, 2013, the House finally passed
VAWA amending federal law to restore limited tribal jurisdiction over non-
Indian abusers committing such acts in Indian country.

The inclusion of the Tribal Title in 2005[73] was historically significant
because it represented for the first time in U.S. history that Congress
recognized the severity of the violence against Native women and the need
to enact federal legislation supporting increased protections. In 2013,
Congress once again reaffirmed the legal relationship and commitment that
the United States has to Indian tribes and the safety of Native women.
VAWA 2013 built upon the 2005 finding that the unique legal relationship
between the United States and Indian tribes creates a federal trust
responsibility to assist tribal governments in safeguarding the lives of Indian
women. VAWA 2013 further strengthened the capacity of Indian tribes to

exercise their sovereign authority to respond to violent crimes against Indian women by clarifying tribal criminal and civil authority.

This chapter provides a review of each section of the VAWA Safety for Indian Women Title and the importance of the provisions to the safety of Native women. Since the enactment of the Tribal Title in 2005, many examples demonstrate how the specific provisions have increased the safety of American Indian women, the safety of law enforcement officers responding to VAWA crimes, and systemic reforms to enhance tribal and federal governmental responses to such crimes.

Identifying and addressing outstanding areas of unmet need to the extent possible guided the drafting of the 2005 Safety for Indian Women Title. It is important to note that not all of the NCAI Task Force's recommendations were enacted in 2005. For example, in 2003 the Task Force proposed that jurisdiction be restored over non-Indians committing domestic violence, sexual assault, dating violence, and violations of orders of protections, but this recommendation was not included until passage of the VAWA 2013. Addressing additional barriers to the safety of Native women through legal reforms under future VAWA reauthorizations will be an ongoing task for the national movement for the safety of Native women. Understanding the relationship of each VAWA reauthorization as interrelated stepping-stones to safety is essential to creating the changes needed. The following four categories describe the reforms enacted under VAWA 2005 and VAWA 2013, Safety for Indian Women Title.

Government-to-Government Relations

To assure preservation of proper governmental relations between the United States and Indian nations regarding VAWA 2005 implementation, Title IX statutorily established the Deputy Director for Tribal Affairs. Additionally, it explicitly required the Department of Justice (USDOJ) and Department of Health and Human Services (HHS) to conduct annual consultations with Indian tribes on statutorily defined categories. VAWA 2013 expanded the VAWA consultation mandate to include the Department of Interior and provided additional safeguards to support the consultation process and implementation of this provision.

Federal Code Amendments

The VAWA 2005 Tribal Title amended several federal codes including: the Firearms Possession Prohibitions of VAWA 2000 to include tribal court convictions; the Indian Law Enforcement Reform Act to include misdemeanor arrest authority; and the Federal Criminal Information Databases to allow Indian nations database access to enter and obtain information. VAWA 2005 also enacted a new federal statute making Domestic Assault by an Habitual Offender a federal felony offense that carries an enhanced penalty for repeat misdemeanor offenders. The VAWA 2013 amendments to the Tribal Title are historic in terms of tribal jurisdiction over non-Indians, particularly involving restoration of limited inherent tribal criminal jurisdiction over non-Indians and reaffirming the civil authority of tribal courts to issue and enforce orders of protection over all persons, Indian and non-Indian alike. VAWA 2013 also created a new federal offense of Assault of a Spouse, Intimate Partner, or Dating Partner by Strangling or Suffocating. Additionally, it amended several federal assault statutes which raised sentencing to higher levels found in many states, and expanded the federal assault statute to include injury to a spouse, intimate partner, or dating partner.

Research and Information Access

In the research area, the 2005 Tribal Title provided for a National Institute of Justice (NIJ) national baseline study on rates of violence against Indian women and a Centers for Disease Control and Prevention (CDC) study on the costs of injury to Indian women due to violence. The VAWA 2013 extended the time period of the national baseline study and funding authorization for the research study. In the area related to information access, the 2005 Tribal Title authorized the USDOJ to develop and maintain a national tribal sex offender and protection order registry to enhance the ability of tribal governments and law enforcement agencies to respond to violence against Indian women on tribal lands. The 2013 Tribal Title continued funding authorization for the national tribal registry through fiscal year 2018.

Increased Resources

The 2005 Tribal Title created the Grants to Indian Tribal Governments Program (GITGP), which lifted programmatic restrictions to allow Indian tribes to determine the appropriate governmental strategies according to their respective forms of governance. The title clarified that Indian tribes are not required under this grant program to provide a match for the federal funds. The 2013 Tribal Title amended this grant program to add two additional purposes for which Indian tribes can use grant funds: sex trafficking and reform efforts to address the five VAWA crimes. The Tribal Title also required that entities having expertise in tribal law, customary practices, and federal Indian law provide technical assistance to Indian tribes and organizations. The Office on Violence Against Women (OVW) entities that provide technical assistance to the tribal grant programs typically are tribal experts.

Findings
VAWA 2005 §901

In 2005, with the goal of broadening VAWA to comprehensively address issues impacting the safety of Native women, Congressional champions for Indian tribes worked closely with the NCAI Task Force and tribal leaders to better understand the epidemic of violence against Native women and to support inclusion in VAWA 2005 required provisions to address such violence. The Senate Committee on Indian Affairs, led by then Senator Byron Dorgan (ND) and Senator Tim Johnson (SD), hosted several hearings on the need for law enforcement reform as well as a specific hearing on violence against Indian women. During these hearings, advocates for the safety of Native women, tribal leaders, and policy experts presented testimony on the violence as well as the need for reforms to federal law and policies.

Native women who traveled to Washington, DC, from their tribal homelands in the months prior to the passage of VAWA 2005 included Karen Artichoker (Oglala Sioux), Tammy Young (Sitka, AK), Dorma Sahneyah (Hopi Tewa, AZ), and Bonnie Clairmont (Ho-Chunk, WI). In addition to the oral testimony provided, many tribal organizations submitted written statements, including the National Congress of American Indians, the Alaska Native Women's Coalition, Sacred Circle, Qualla Women's Justice Alliance, Tohono O'odham Nation Department of Public Safety, and the Navajo Nation. It is to the credit of these grassroots tribal advocates and Indian tribes that the Senate Committee on Indian Affairs developed a strong record for understanding the nature and prevalence of violence against Native women living on tribal lands.

In passage of the Safety for Indian Women Title, Congress relied on the written and oral statements and other information gathered during the hearings conducted by the Senate Committee on Indian Affairs. The statistics listed in the Findings sections of the Tribal Title were brought to light for the Committee, Congress, and the nation. Since passage in 2005, additional statistics have been revealed reaffirming the urgent need for immediate reform of the justice system to enhance the safety of Native women. The original Congressional findings of 2005 were not amended during the 2013 reauthorization and remain unchanged.

The six Congressional findings stand as a strong national statement of the current epidemic of violence endangering the physical safety and quality of life of Native women. These findings provided the justification for creation of Title IX and amendments to the Violence Against Women Act of 1994 and 2000. Findings 1–4 are statistics from federal research that highlight the nature and extent of violence against Indian women. Finding 5 is a conclusion reported by the U.S. Civil Rights Commission in its report, "A Quiet Crisis: Federal Funding and Unmet Needs in Indian Country." Finding 6 articulates the legal responsibility of the United States to Indian tribes in safeguarding the lives of Indian women.

VAWA 2005. §901. Findings.

Congress finds that—
(1) 1 out of every 3 Indian (including Alaska Native) women are raped in their lifetimes;
(2) Indian women experience 7 sexual assaults per 1,000, compared with 4 per 1,000 among Black Americans, 3 per 1,000 among Caucasians, 2 per 1,000 among Hispanic women, and 1 per 1,000 among Asian women;
(3) Indian women experience the violent crime of battering at a rate of 23.2 per 1,000, compared with 8 per 1,000 among Caucasian women;
(4) during the period 1979 through 1992, homicide was the third leading cause of death of Indian females aged 15 to 34, and 75 percent were killed by family members or acquaintances;
(5) Indian tribes require additional criminal justice and victim services resources to respond to violent assaults against women; and
(6) the unique legal relationship of the United States to Indian tribes creates a federal trust responsibility to assist tribal governments in safeguarding the lives of Indian women.

The Congressional purposes for the enactment of the Safety for Indian Women Title provides an overview of the goals Congress intended be accomplished by Title IX of the VAWA 2005. The three purpose areas also provide clarity for the implementation of the Act. It links the decrease of violence against Indian women to the increased capacity of Indian tribes to exercise their sovereign authority to protect Indian women and hold perpetrators accountable for their crimes.

Congress established these three purpose areas specifically to support the provisions contained in the Safety for Indian Women Title. The inclusion of language recognizing the "sovereign authority to respond to violent crimes committed against Indian women" is extremely significant to self-governance. The concurrent authority of Indian tribes and the United States under the Major Crimes Act created confusion for justice agencies responding to violent crimes against Indian women. Particularly, in crimes of sexual assault, an inaccurate interpretation has resulted in a public myth that Indian tribes lack jurisdictional authority to respond to the crime of rape. This language and other language contained in the VAWA 2005 and 2013 clarified this confusion. Furthermore, it supports the sovereign authority of Indian tribes to protect Native women and sets forth the proper government-to-government relationship of the USDOJ to Indian tribes in the implementation of the provisions and administration of the programs contained in the title.

VAWA 2005. §902. Purposes.

The purposes of this title are:
(1) to decrease the incidence of violent crimes against Indian women;
(2) to strengthen the capacity of Indian tribes to exercise their sovereign authority to respond to violent crimes committed against Indian women; and
(3) to ensure that perpetrators of violent crimes committed against Indian women are held accountable for their criminal behavior.

In 2000, President Clinton signed Executive Order 1175 on "Consultation and Coordination with Indian Tribal Governments."[74] In 2009, President Obama continued this directive signing a Memorandum on Tribal Consultation pronouncing tribal consultations "a critical ingredient of a sound and productive federal-tribal relationship."[75] In this broader context, Congress established in VAWA 2005 and strengthened in VAWA 2013 a specific mandate requiring an annual tribal consultation addressing violence against Native women.

The VAWA 2005 Safety for Indian Women Title mandates that the U.S. Departments of Justice (USDOJ) and Health and Human Services (HHS) each consult annually with Indian nations on issues concerning the safety of Indian women. It required that the United States solicit recommendations during these annual consultations from Indian tribes concerning three specific areas:

1. Administering tribal funds and programs;
2. Enhancing the safety of Indian women from domestic violence, dating violence, sexual assault, and stalking; and,
3. Strengthening the federal response to such violent crimes.

VAWA 2013 further extends this mandate to addressing tribal leaders' expressed concerns on the consultation process. The 2013 amendments increase the likelihood that by engaging in mutual dialogue as governments the legal and policy roadblocks to the safety of Native women will be removed. In drafting the 2005 Tribal Title, the consultation process was viewed as an essential way to involve the participation of tribal governments in the implementation of VAWA, which in turn leads to strengthened internal tribal capacity to increase safety for Native women.

The NCAI Task Force understood that for VAWA to increase systematic protections for Native women, Indian nations would need to identify barriers and implement solutions that will enhance their capacity as governments to protect women. An annual consultation on the highest level of legal and policy issues between the United States and Indian nations as governments was seen as an essential safeguard to the successful implementation of VAWA.

The historic amendments of VAWA 2013 confirm that the inclusion of a separate annual consultation with Indian tribes on safety for Native women is, and will continue to be, critical to successful implementation of VAWA. This nation-to-nation interaction provides an avenue for tribal governments and the United States to discuss matters that at the broadest level impact the safety of Indian women. It provides an opportunity to examine and address important issues that impact all Indian nations in providing safety for women.

The VAWA 2013 tribal amendments are the result of concerns raised during the consultation process since 2006. Over the last seven years, tribal leaders have raised and engaged the USDOJ leadership in dialogue on the most serious roadblocks to the safety of Native women and on issues impacting the ability of Indian tribes to protect women. VAWA 2013 amendments to the VAWA 2005 consultation mandate are outlined below.

In preparation for each of the annual consultations, the NCAI Task Force coordinated a preparatory caucus for tribal leaders, during which tribal leaders received a briefing and review of outstanding issues concerning the safety of Indian women. Following each caucus, a developed list of recommendations regarding the implementation of VAWA was provided to the USDOJ and the White House.

For each VAWA consultation, the National Indigenous Women's Resource Center in partnership with the Task Force publish a special edition of the *Restoration* magazine. This special consultation edition provides tribal leaders with a written outline of past consultation matters. It provides a review of the tribal provisions contained in the Tribal Title and previous concerns and recommendations made to the USDOJ addressing the three statutory mandated areas. Lastly, recommendations are provided to the USDOJ that could significantly increase the capacity of Indian tribes to assist victims of domestic violence, dating violence, sexual assault, and now, sex trafficking.

During the initial years (2006–2008), following enactment of the VAWA annual tribal consultation mandate, tribal leadership raised numerous concerns that the USDOJ was not fully implementing the mandate. Since 2009, the consultation process organized by OVW has improved each year with the increased attendance of USDOJ leadership, issuance of the required consultation report to Congress and made available online,[76] and a pre-consultation process to determine date, location, and consultation issues. While the VAWA 2005 consultation mandate included the Secretary of the Department of Health and Human Services (HHS), the Department was engaged in ongoing annual consultation with Indian tribes. While continuing this practice, the HHS also, since 2011, attends the VAWA-mandated annual consultation. The annual consultation established under the VAWA 2005 is now institutionalized and provides a process to annually review and monitor critical issues concerning the safety of Native women.

VAWA 2013 Amendments to the VAWA 2005 Consultation Mandate Require:

- The Attorney General provides 120 days' notice to Indian tribes of the date, time, and location of the annual consultation.
- The Secretary of Interior attends the annual consultation.
- The Attorney General submits to Congress an annual report that:
  - Contains the recommendations made by Indian tribes during the year covered by the report
  - Describes actions taken during the year to respond to recommendations made during the year or a previous year
  - Describes how the Attorney General will work in coordination and collaboration with Indian tribes, the Secretary of Health and Human Services, and the Secretary of the Interior to address the recommendations
- Sex trafficking is added to the list of items to be addressed at the consultation.

Annual USDOJ VAWA Consultations 2006–2013

Date	Location	Highest USDOJ HHS Official
September 19, 2006	Shakopee, Mdewakanton Sioux Community, MN	OVW Director Diane Stuart
September 19, 2007	Sandia Pueblo, NM	Acting OVW Director Mary Beth Buchanan
December 10, 2008	Agua Caliente Band of Cahuilla Indians, Palm Springs, CA	OVW Director Cindy Dyer
October 30, 2009	St. Paul, MN	USDOJ Associate Attorney General Tom Perrelli; HHS* Director Marylouise Kelly

October 4, 2010	Kalispel Indian Tribe Airway Heights, WA	USDOJ Associate Attorney General Tom Perrelli
December 15, 2011	Santa Ana Pueblo, NM	OVW Director Susan Carbon; HHS Director Marylouise Kelly
October 2, 2012	Tulsa, OK	OVW Acting Director Bea Hanson; HHS Director Marylouise Kelly
November 14, 2013	Washington, DC	Associate Attorney General Tony West

*Department of Health and Human Services, Family Violence Prevention Division, Family and Youth Services Bureau, Administration for Children and Families (ACF)

VAWA 2005. §903. Consultation.

(a) In General—The Attorney General shall conduct annual consultations with Indian tribal governments concerning the federal administration of tribal funds and programs established under this Act, the Violence Against Women Act of 1994 (Title IV of Public Law 103-322; 108 Stat. 1902), and the Violence Against Women Act of 2000 (division B of Public Law 106-386; 114 Stat. 1491).

(b) Recommendations—During consultations under subsection (a), the Secretary of the Department of Health and Human Services and the Attorney General shall solicit recommendations from Indian tribes concerning—

(1) administering tribal funds and programs;

(2) enhancing the safety of Indian women from domestic violence, dating violence, sexual assault, and stalking; and

(3) strengthening the federal response to such violent crimes.

VAWA 2013. §903. Consultation.

Section 903 of the Violence Against Women and Department of Justice Reauthorization Act of 2005 (42 U.S.C. 14045d) is amended—
(1) in subsection (a)—
(A) by striking "and the Violence Against Women Act of 2000" and inserting ", the Violence Against Women Act of 2000"; and
(B) by inserting ", and the Violence Against Women Reauthorization Act of 2013" before the period at the end;
(2) in subsection (b)—
(A) in the matter preceding paragraph (1), by striking "Secretary of the Department of Health and Human Services" and inserting "Secretary of Health and Human Services, the Secretary of Interior," and
(B) in paragraph (2), by striking "and stalking" and inserting "stalking, and sex trafficking"; and (3) by adding at the end the following:
"(c) Annual Report.—The Attorney General shall submit to Congress an annual report on the annual consultations required under subsection (a) that—
"(1) contains the recommendations made under subsection (b) by Indian tribes during the year covered by the report;
"(2) describes actions taken during the year covered by the report to respond to recommendations made under subsection (b) during the year or a previous year; and
"(3) describes how the Attorney General will work in coordination and collaboration with Indian tribes, the Secretary of Health and Human Services, and the Secretary of the Interior to address the recommendations made under subsection (b).
"(d) Notice.—Not later than 120 days before the date of a consultation under subsection (a), the Attorney General shall notify tribal leaders of the date, time, and location of the consultation."

Analysis and Research on Violence Against Indian Women
VAWA 2005 §904 and VAWA 2013 §907

VAWA 2005 §904(a) directs the Attorney General, acting through the National Institute of Justice (NIJ), in consultation with the Director of the Office on Violence Against Women (OVW) to conduct a national baseline study on violence against American Indian women. This section was enacted to address the lack of research on violence against Indian women and to develop a more comprehensive understanding of this violence and its effect on Indian women across the social spectrum and throughout their lifetimes. The NIJ in partnership with OVW has initiated implementation of this important statute.

NIJ under Section (a) of the statute developed a program of research to fully implement the goals of the statute. The purpose of the research program is to: examine violence against Native women (including domestic violence, dating violence, sexual assault, stalking, and murder) and identify factors that place Native women at risk for victimization; evaluate the effectiveness of federal, state, tribal, and local responses to violence against Native women; and propose recommendations to improve effectiveness of these responses.

NIJ's program of research on violence against Indian women is designed to: (1) provide for the first time an accurate reporting of violence against American Indian and Alaska Native women in tribal communities, (2) provide reliable valid estimates of the scope of the problem, and (3) identify problems and possible solutions in dealing with these issues that may lead to public policies and prevention strategies designed to decrease the incidence of violent crimes committed against Native women. Results from these studies are expected to help establish and enhance justice systems that successfully restore victim safety and promote healing.

Under VAWA 2005, Section 904(b) created an Attorney General–appointed Federal Advisory Task Force on Violence Against Women to assist in the development and implementation of the program of research and also guide implementation of the recommendations made to Congress under the study. Attorney General Eric Holder established the Task Force on March 31, 2008,[77] and re-chartered the Task Force on July 26, 2012. Working closely with the NIJ, the 2008 Task Force guided the initial conceptualization of the NIJ program of research and provided written recommendations at the end of its two-year appointment by the Attorney General in 2010. On the importance of the research and analysis component of VAWA, the Task Force stated:

The lack of understanding of ... legal barriers contained in this complex body of federal Indian law was the basis for a section of the Tribal Title to mandate analysis and research of the federal, state, tribal, and local systems responsible for safeguarding the lives of Indian women. If VAWA is to enhance the safety of Indian women, it is critical to understand these systems that are charged with the responsibility of responding to VAWA-related crimes. These legal barriers ultimately impact the ability of Indian women to live free of violence and the authority of Indian tribes to safeguard the lives of the citizens of their respective nations. The well-documented under reporting of these crimes by Indian women is illustrative of the failure of the systems to be evaluated.

The statute acknowledged that such research would require the close guidance of Indian tribes, advocates providing services to Indian women, and other policy experts and mandated that a task force be created to guide the development and implementation of the research project.[78]

Following reauthorization of VAWA 2013, the Attorney General created a second federal advisory committee that is working in close partnership with the NIJ in the implementation of the Section 904(a) program of research.

VAWA 2013 amended the VAWA 2005 research provision to clarify that Congress intended Alaska Native women to be included in the program of research, add sex trafficking to the type of violence to be examined, and extend the authorized funding level at $1 million annually until 2018. Under Section (b), NIJ is currently working in close partnership with the second Task Force established under Section (b) of the statute to assist in the development and implementation of the study and program of research.

VAWA 2005. §904. Analysis and Research on Violence Against Indian Women.

(a) National Baseline Study—
(1) In General—The National Institute of Justice, in consultation with the Office on Violence Against Women,

shall conduct a national baseline study to examine violence against Indian women in Indian country.

(2) Scope—

(A) In General—The study shall examine violence committed against Indian women, including—

   (i) domestic violence;

   (ii) dating violence;

   (iii) sexual assault;

   (iv) stalking; and

   (v) murder.

(B) Evaluation—The study shall evaluate the effectiveness of federal, state, tribal, and local responses to the violations described in subparagraph (A) committed against Indian women.

(C) Recommendations—The study shall propose recommendations to improve the effectiveness of federal, state, tribal, and local responses to the violation described in subparagraph (A) committed against Indian women.

(3) Task Force—

(A) In General—The Attorney General, acting through the Director of the Office on Violence Against Women, shall establish a task force to assist in the development and implementation of the study under paragraph (1) and guide implementation of the recommendation in paragraph (2)(C).

(B) Members—The Director shall appoint to the task force representatives from—

   (i) national tribal domestic violence and sexual assault nonprofit organizations;

   (ii) tribal governments; and

   (iii) the national tribal organizations.

(4) Report—Not later than 2 years after the date of enactment of this Act, the Attorney General shall submit to the Committee on Indian Affairs of the Senate, the Committee on the Judiciary of the Senate, and the Committee on the Judiciary of the House of Representatives a report that describes the study.

VAWA 2013. §907. Analysis and Research on Violence Against Indian Women.

(a) In General.—Section 904(a) of the Violence Against Women and Department of Justice Reauthorization Act of 2005 (42 U.S.C. 3796gg–10 note) is amended—
(1) in paragraph (1)—
(A) by striking "The National" and inserting "Not later than 2 years after the date of enactment of the Violence Against Women Reauthorization Act of 2013, the National"; and
(B) by inserting "and in Native villages (as defined in section 3 of the Alaska Native Claims Settlement Act (43 U.S.C. 1602))" before the period at the end;
(2) in paragraph (2)(A)—
(A) in clause (iv), by striking "and" at the end;
(B) in clause (v), by striking the period at the end and inserting "; and"; and
(C) by adding at the end the following: "(vi) sex trafficking.";
(3) in paragraph (4), by striking "this Act" and inserting "the Violence Against Women Reauthorization Act of 2013"; and
(4) in paragraph (5), by striking "this section $1,000,000 for each of fiscal years 2007 and 2008" and inserting "this subsection $1,000,000 for each of fiscal years 2014 and 2015".
(b) Authorization of Appropriations.—Section 905(b)(2) of the Violence Against Women and Department of Justice Reauthorization Act of 2005 (28 U.S.C. 534 note) is amended by striking "fiscal years 2007 through 2011" and inserting "fiscal years 2014 through 2018".

Section 905(a) of VAWA amended the federal code to require the Attorney General to permit Indian law enforcement agencies, in the cases of domestic violence, dating violence, sexual assault, and stalking, to enter information into, and obtain information from, federal criminal information databases. This amendment permitting Indian law enforcement agencies access to and entry into federal criminal information databases was a tremendous step forward in creating safety for Indian women.

Passage of the Tribal Law and Order Act of 2010 amended the law once more to provide that "the Attorney General shall ensure that tribal law enforcement officials that meet applicable federal or state requirements be permitted access to national crime information databases." [80] This confirmed Congress' intent that tribal law enforcement be granted full access to federal criminal information databases. Under the TLOA amendment, Congress broadened tribal access beyond the four crimes specified under VAWA 2005.

Tribal law enforcement access to federal criminal databases is a foundational element of an effective law enforcement response to tribal victims of domestic violence, sexual assault, and other VAWA-related crimes. The National Crime Information Center (NCIC) maintains 21 national data files many of which are directly related to the emergency response of tribal law enforcement to assist victims. Law enforcement responding to a domestic violence incident with NCIC access can verify a protection order, whether the suspect is a convicted sex offender in violation of registration requirements, is prohibited from possessing firearms, has an outstanding warrant, or is in violation of terms of parole. In addition to enhancing the immediate response of law enforcement, NCIC access provides essential information to alert tribal justice officials and trigger additional federal felony charges such as the Federal Tribal Habitual Offender. Lastly, actual full access of tribal law enforcement to NCIC is essential to officer safety in the performance of their daily duties that often place them in dangerous situations.

Not only is access to NCIC files essential, but also critical to the safety of Native women, all victims, and law enforcement is the ability to enter tribal information. Often perpetrators of domestic violence travel from one tribe to another. The ability to alert other Indian tribes of an abuser's violence, convictions, and other lifesaving information requires the capability to not only obtain but also to enter information into federal criminal databases.

In response to concerns raised during annual USDOJ VAWA consultations about the lack of implementation of Section 905(a), the USDOJ reviewed the lack of access issue. Based on its finding that certain Indian tribes wanted and did not have access to the NCIC, a pilot project was launched to assist tribes. Under the pilot project, 22 Indian tribes were identified as lacking the required setup for NCIC access, and the USDOJ installed the required equipment to gain access. Where the state government would not grant Indian tribes access through the state system, the USDOJ provided an alternative means of access through the federal system called the Justice Telecommunications System (JUST).

The Sycuan Band of the Kumeyaay Nation, located in San Diego County, California, was one of 22 Indian tribes that gained direct, full NCIC access with the assistance of the USDOJ. Bill Denke, Chief of the Sycuan Tribal Police Department provided the following testimony before the Indian Law and Order Commission:

> The California Attorney General's Office has opined that tribal law enforcement agencies in California do not qualify for access into the state's system, the California Law Enforcement Telecommunications System (CLETS) under California's government code. The hang-up is the requirement for the law enforcement agency to be defined as a public agency. In California, CLETS is the gateway to national databases through the NCIC. As a workaround to this problem, in 2010 under the direction of Attorney General Holder and facilitated by the Office of Tribal Justice, FBI-vetted tribal agencies were sponsored by the Justice Department for connectivity to NCIC and the National Law Enforcement Telecommunications System (NLETS). NLETS provides the interstate sharing of law enforcement information; however, not all CLETS information can be accessed through NLETS. Examples of inaccessible state information is, but not limited to: parole and probations status, local warrants, photographs, detailed motor vehicle information, firearms files, and be-on-the-lookout information. Although, the tribal law enforcement agencies that currently have access to NCIC and NLETS initially hit a snag with accessing state information via NLETS, California Attorney General Kamala Harris' staff along with the BIA Office of Justice Services Deputy Bureau Director

Cruzan's staff have collaborated to fix it, thus allowing Justice Department–sponsored tribal law enforcement agencies with SLEC officers access. It is very important to note though, until vetted tribal law enforcement officers have full access to CLETS, there will remain a huge officer safety issue in California's Indian country. With that being said, I strongly encourage the collaboration between the California Attorney General's Office and the BIA Office of Justice Services to continue in an effort to find resolve. And for the local sheriffs who are assisting with this, I commend.

The pace at which the Department of Justice is working to resolve issues related to full access of tribal law enforcement agencies to federal criminal information databases is an outstanding concern raised during annual VAWA consultations. Full implementation of Section 905(a) has been particularly challenging. A framing paper released by OVW for the 2013 annual VAWA consultation further clarifies certain implementation issues and questions regarding Section 905(a).[81]

VAWA 2005 §905(a). Access to Federal Databases.

(a) Access to Federal Criminal Information Databases—
Section 534 of Title 28, United States Code, is amended—
(1) by redesignating subsection (d) as subsection (e); and
 (2) by inserting after subsection (c) the following:
"(d) Indian Law Enforcement Agencies. The Attorney General shall permit Indian law enforcement agencies, in cases of domestic violence, dating violence, sexual assault, and stalking, to enter information into federal criminal information databases and to obtain information from the databases."

TLOA 2010 §233. Access to National Criminal Information Databases.[82]

(a) Access to National Criminal Information Databases.—
Section 534 of Title 28, United States Code, is amended—
(1) in subsection (a)(4), by inserting "Indian tribes," after "the States,";

(2) by striking subsection (d) and inserting the following:
"(d) Indian Law Enforcement Agencies.—The Attorney General shall permit tribal and Bureau of Indian Affairs law enforcement agencies—
"(1) to access and enter information into federal criminal information databases; and
"(2) to obtain information from the databases.";
(3) by redesignating the second subsection (e) as subsection (f); and
(4) in paragraph (2) of subsection (f) (as redesignated by paragraph (3)), in the matter preceding subparagraph (A), by inserting ", tribal," after "federal".
(b) Requirement.—
(1) In General.—The Attorney General shall ensure that tribal law enforcement officials that meet applicable federal or state requirements be permitted access to national crime information databases.
(2) Sanctions.—For purpose of sanctions for noncompliance with requirements of, or misuse of, national crime information databases and information obtained from those databases, a tribal law enforcement agency or official shall be treated as federal law enforcement agency or official.
(3) NCIC.—Each tribal justice official serving an Indian tribe with criminal jurisdiction over Indian country shall be considered to be an authorized law enforcement official for purposes of access to the National Crime Information Center of the Federal Bureau of Investigation.

National Tribal Sex Offender and Order of Protection Registry VAWA 2005 §905(b)

The ability of Indian tribes to access the national tribal registry would enable tribes to protect their communities from transient habitual perpetrators who prey on Indian women. Abusers who batter and rape Native women often move from one Indian tribe to another. These perpetrators, when held accountable by family or law enforcement, move to different tribal communities where members often are unaware of the danger the abuser poses to the community.

In 2003, the grassroots tribal advocacy movement witnessing this pattern worked to educate elected leaders, and as a result Congress authorized the creation of a National Tribal Sex Offender and Order of Protection Registry in 2005. The tribal registry is intended to make available lifesaving information to protect Native women and their tribal communities from such offenders. The importance of the registry is reflected in the words of Florence Choyou.

Florence Choyou

I am the mother of Monica Choyou, who was murdered by her supposed boyfriend whom she only knew for a month-and-a-half. He was a Native but not a member of the Hopi tribe. Monica passed away May 5, 2009. We can't be definite, but her body was found on May 10, at approximately 8:30 in the morning.

We had gone to Peach Springs, AZ, to be with my only brother who was terminally ill. We were to have a family meeting and to be with him for the last time. So we left on a Saturday morning, and I remember my daughter that morning being so happy when she got up. She said, "Mom are you going right now?" I told her yes. I did not know I would not see her again. I can just picture her standing there at the window looking at me like she wanted to say something. She just had a look of being anxious in some way. I remember she waived at me and I waved back.

I called home on Monday and Monica answered the phone and said, "Mom, we are okay." She sounded very happy. My daughter had a green thumb. My husband has health issues, so Monica was the one who planted our corn, beans, and such. She had been gardening that day when I last spoke to her on the phone.

That night the police were called because of an argument and her boyfriend was under the influence. When they got to her house my daughter told the two police officers that she would take care of her boyfriend so that he would mellow out. He is not a member of our tribe and the police should have taken him in for being under the influence.

When we got home from Peach Springs, I asked my younger daughter if Monica had come over.

She said no.

Later my younger daughter said, "Mom, I think you better call the police. I went over to Monica's and there is blood all over. The door is busted. The window is busted. Something happened there." So my grandson, my youngest daughter, and my husband went over to Monica's. I stayed at home with the grandkids.

About 20 minutes later they came back and described what happened. "I don't know, but it looks like someone was slaughtered in that house. There is blood all over the walls, the windows; everything is turned upside down. The window is completely off the window frame. I found it near the outhouse. The door is bashed in. Her mattress is saturated with blood. The mirrors are broke. It is just a mess. I looked around and I saw handprints in the sand like someone dragged someone. I could only track it so far because of the rocks. I don't know what happened but I am calling the police."

A tribal police officer came in about 20 minutes and asked us questions. When I mentioned her boyfriend's name, he quit writing and said, "That name sounds familiar. I arrested him before and found he was banished from Laguna and Zuni. He did something similar. He was violent and injured someone." When the police officer came back, he said they were going to start tracking early in the morning. When I asked what does that mean, he said, "Have you been over there?" And I said no. For some reason I just could not go to her house. There was something holding me back.

The next morning at about four o'clock, the dogs were barking outside and woke me. So I got up and looked outside and seen all these people. Some were on horseback and some were on foot. There were all these police officers in a row just walking. I went over to my daughter's house but there were so many police cars, black SUVs, and white vans that we couldn't get through. Police and crime scene tape blocked the area.

We live in a canyon where there are a lot of trails and fields. And I kept saying to myself, "My daughter is there somewhere." She is okay. She is alright. My daughter's house is in a ravine and not very many people even know there is a house there. We call it the Garden of Eden because it is so green; there are different fruit trees like apples, peaches, and pears. Monica stayed in this beautiful garden.

I remember seeing a white transport down at the bottom of the ravine and saw other police down at the wash, maybe six men. I asked myself, "What are they doing down there?" I was walking down and when I got so far, a man stopped me and asked who I was and if I owned this property. He questioned me and kept asking me all these questions about my daughter. Later I remember coming around my car and I looked down at the wash. I saw four men carrying a bag and they went under the apple tree, and I said wonder what that is. We were ready to leave and a man motioned for us to stop. One finally said they found a body. I got angry and said, "Is it my daughter? Is it my daughter?"

My world came to an end.

The man who violently took Monica's life received three years and will be released soon. Before coming to our reservation, he was banished from two other nearby reservations for violence. If we had only known of his violence, she might still be alive. The tribal registry might have saved her life.

—Florence Choyou

Congress included Section 905(b) in VAWA 2005 to partially address that lack of availability of information regarding tribal orders of protection and convicted sex offenders. Section 905(b) directs the Attorney General to contract with any interested Indian tribe, tribal organization, or tribal nonprofit organization to develop and maintain a national tribal sex offender and tribal protection order registry. The National Tribal Registry was intended to provide all federally recognized Indian tribes the ability to enter lifesaving information into a national registry. Currently, only the domestic violence protection orders of 12 tribes are being entered into the NCIC National Order of Protection Registry.

A separate tribal registry is necessary because administrative barriers currently delay and may also prevent the inclusion of tribal data into the National Sex Offender Public Registry and the National Order of Protection Registry. Such barriers prevent full participation of Indian tribes in national information database systems and also prevent full access of law enforcement agencies to lifesaving critical information.

The creation of a National Tribal Registry designed for Indian tribes to enter and access information regarding orders of protection and convicted sex offenders has the potential to enhance the everyday safety of Indian women. All federally recognized Indian tribes opting to participate will have timely access to lifesaving information. The design of the registry need not include state and federal requirements. It has the potential to streamline administration and participation costs, which may hinder full participation of Indian tribes, which in turn, often results in a lack of full law enforcement agency access to critical lifesaving information maintained in federal information databases.

In 2008, OVW hosted a focus group on developing the tribal registry systems. Participants included a wide number of experts, including tribal law enforcement, advocates for tribal women, and USDOJ agencies like the FBI and federal prosecutors. During the 2010 consultation, OVW reported it would issue the solicitation and contract with an interested entity to develop the National Tribal Order of Protection Registry. A solicitation was issued following the 2012 consultation, but OVW determined that no applicant met the requirements. At the time of this publication, the contract to establish the tribal registry has not been awarded.

In terms of the tribal sex offender registry, OVW is exploring releasing that component at a later date pending discussions with the DOJ Office of Sex Offender Sentencing, Monitoring, Apprehending, Registering, and Tracking (the SMART Office). This is important given the intersection of the SMART Office's work to implement the Adam Walsh Act.

The effectiveness of any database depends on infrastructure development, timely entry of required information, and the ability to maintain correct, updated information. Tribal information entry into national registries that is delayed or inaccurate can place a Native woman at immediate risk. A separate tribal registry was considered a necessity during the passage of VAWA 2005 due to above-described administrative barriers.

Following passage of the Tribal Registry provision, the Adam Walsh Act became law, further complicating the issue of the participation of Indian tribes in a national sex offender registry. All Indian tribes located in states having been granted concurrent jurisdiction with Indian tribes under

PL 280 or similar jurisdiction cannot operate a tribal sex offender registry under the Sex Offender Registration and Notification Act (SORNA), which is a key component of the Adam Walsh Act. Currently, many of these state governments are not in compliance with SORNA, which negatively impacts the ability of the Indian tribes located in these states to register sex offenders under SORNA. Ironically, while 33 Indian tribes are SORNA compliant, only 15 states are in compliance. A majority of states, where Indian tribes are located, are missing from the list of SORNA-compliant states.

VAWA 2005. §905(b). National Tribal Sex Offender and Order of Protection Registry.

(b) Tribal Registry—
(1) Establishment—The Attorney General shall contract with any interested Indian tribe, tribal organization, or tribal nonprofit organization to develop and maintain—
(A) a national tribal sex offender registry; and
(B) a tribal protection order registry containing civil and criminal orders of protection issued by Indian tribes and participating jurisdictions.
(2) Authorization of appropriations—There is an authorized appropriation to carry out this section of $1,000,000 for each of fiscal years 2007 through 2011, to remain available until expended.

Grants to Indian Tribal Governments Program
VAWA 2005 §906 and VAWA 2013 §901

Prior to reauthorization of VAWA in 2005, Indian tribes were eligible to apply for funding under various VAWA grant programs; however, separate application and reporting mechanisms created a burdensome process. VAWA 2005 statutorily combined tribal set-asides from seven different grant programs into a single program called the Grants to Indian Tribal Governments Program (GITGP).

Since fiscal year 2007, OVW has issued a GITGP solicitation that streamlines the application and funding distribution process to Indian tribes. The purpose of creating the GITGP, a single grant program, was to enhance the ability of Indian tribes to access funding to address domestic violence, sexual assault, dating violence, and stalking. The establishment of this program was an important step forward in expanding access of Indian tribes to critical funding.

The lack of services available to Native women on tribal lands places them at increased risks of repeated violence that negatively impacts their quality of life. In particular, the lack of victim services often translates to not having a safe place to sleep, food, health services to treat sustained injuries and deal with rape associated trauma, and 911 or law enforcement services to stop another beating or rape. Furthermore, if the woman has children, these circumstances typically are compounded and often appear insurmountable. The experience of Cherrah Giles, former second speaker of the Muscogee Creek Nation and tribal council member for more than a decade, highlights the impact lack of services may have on a Native woman's daily life.

Cherrah Giles

Hensci (Hello)! My name is Cherrah Giles and I am from the Thlikatchka (Broken Arrow Tribal Town) and of the Fuswv (Bird Clan) from the Muscogee (Creek) Nation located in Oklahoma. I write this letter to you to help shed light on why Native women are in great need of services funded under the VAWA Tribal Government Grant Program.

My words are as a survivor of over 15 years of domestic violence and abuse. The violence perpetrated against me began when I was just a teenager in high school. From the early age of 15, the boy I dated abused me. At a time when I should have experienced the joys of high school and becoming a woman, I experienced violence from being hit, kicked, and punched. I endured humiliating acts from being spit upon, having my hair pulled, a knife pulled on me, cigarettes put out on my face, to full beer cans thrown at my head. I went to high school with bruises and a black eye.

At the time, there were no tribal programs for teens and young women being abused as a result of teen dating violence. I became pregnant at 16 with this same boy and became a teen mom while having to endure the continued abuse. Again, there were no tribal dating violence services for pregnant teens and women like me.

My teenage boyfriend became my husband, and for more than a decade, the hitting, kicking, punching, and humiliation continued. My abuse and abuser remained a part of my life as I transitioned from a teen to an adult woman. Domestic abuse and violence remained a constant as I went from a high school student, to a college and graduate student, and into my professional life as an elected tribal leader and social worker.

My abuse, like the abuse so many Native women endure, was not during one single point in my life but over a long period of time. For some, the violence is endured over a lifetime. Many Native women endure lifelong violence because they get to a place where there seems to be no way to break the cycle of abuse. The abuse becomes a part of everyday life.

What I experienced was a pattern of day-to-day incidents of physical and emotional abuse known as domestic violence. Many of these incidents are considered misdemeanors, but I want to stress that the repeated acts of violence constituted a pattern of ongoing terror in my life. When this abuse is committed by a non-Indian against a Native woman on tribal land, the tribal government has no jurisdiction to hold the abuser accountable. This is a problem and is unacceptable.

I was first elected to tribal council in 2002 when I was 24. As an elected leader of my Nation, I lived a very public life. I attended tribal council meetings, traveled for my Nation, and spoke at hundreds of public events. On numerous occasions, I conducted my professional duties with bruises on my body. I kept these bruises hidden by my clothing, as I feared a stigma of weakness from being a victim. I now understand that my abuser intended these attacks and visible marks on my body to be hidden. Blows to the head, hair pulling, and spitting are just a few of the acts that do not leave visible marks.

It was not until my Nation launched a program for victims of domestic violence that I became more aware that I was a victim of domestic violence. Even as I became more aware, I did not leave my abuser because of my perceived stigma of victims being weak and the embarrassment of living with abuse. The fear of retaliation from trying to break loose from the cycle of abuse was another big factor in not leaving my abusive spouse.

On October 25, 2008, I was beaten and choked. I remember this date because it was three hours before a tribal council meeting. I attended that council meeting with finger and handprints on my neck from being choked. At the council meeting, I kept my head down with my hair pulled forward to try and keep the marks from being seen. It was after that meeting I had my moment of change and I realized it had to stop. I had to get out of this cycle of abuse.

Soon after, I went to my tribal domestic violence program and sought help. I am so grateful that this program was available and that it existed. It helped me to stop the violence in my life, as I now knew the experience of seeking help.

Violence against women is not a traditional value for my tribe. It has never been acceptable. Yet, domestic abuse and violence have diluted our sense of well-being and is counter to our traditional values and beliefs of community love and support. It was not until after I left my abuser that I felt comfortable speaking about it in public, and with family and friends.

I want to tell you that if tribal services geared toward domestic violence had not been available, I'm certain I would not be speaking here today. I'm certain I would have remained in the cycle of abuse with an attitude of "no way out" and accepting of a life of violence put upon me. My life is now in a better place, free of abuse thanks to the aid and assistance from these tribal services.

I also want to share with you the desperate need for rape crisis services. It is estimated one out of three Native women will be raped in her lifetime. My Nation's health system is in the process of establishing better protocols and strengthening the response needs to victims of sexual assault by establishing a Tribal Sexual Assault Nurse Examiner.

Today, many things in my life have changed for the better, but we have so much further to go in order to create tribal communities where Native women can live free of violence.

I survived the violence committed against me for over a decade. I have four beautiful children, two girls and two boys, and a fiancé who shares in my effort to prevent and abolish domestic violence. We work very hard raising my children to understand that domestic violence is not acceptable. Just a few weeks ago, I resigned as Second Speaker of my tribal council to work as the Director of Community and Human Services. My position oversees eight tribal programs, which includes our Family Violence Prevention Program. This change allows me to work directly with our tribal community in the effort to eradicate domestic violence. I feel blessed and so fortunate for the opportunities at hand.

As a victim, I made excuses for my abuser. I think as elected officials we cannot make excuses for abusers. We need to assume the responsibilities placed upon us and create laws that hold offenders accountable and remove the physical and mental burden from those being abused. This responsibility to end the violence against victims in the United States includes violence against Native women.

The Violence Against Women Act in 1994 opened the doors for Native women. It recognized tribal nations as sovereign governments that must be able to protect Native women within their own tribal boundaries. Native women need the services as proposed under the Grants to Indian Tribal Governments Program to access basic services to end the violence and save their lives and the lives of their children and families.

Mvto (Thank you)!
Cherrah Giles
(May 10, 2012)

In 2013, increased public awareness and education by the various tribal women's coalitions regarding sex trafficking of Native women resulted in a broadening by Congress of the purpose areas under the tribal grants program to include this issue. With the inclusion of sex trafficking as a purpose area for Indian tribes under VAWA 2013, it is important now to broaden national attention on the safety of Native women to include sexual exploitation and trafficking.[83] The U.S. government must continue efforts to resolve the jurisdictional maze and egregious discrepancies Native women face in the prosecution of perpetrators committing these heinous crimes. The jurisdictional confusion, government inaction, and other legal and public policy issues barring access to justice for Native women must be eliminated.

VAWA 2005. §906. Grants to Indian Tribal Governments.

(a) Grants—The Attorney General may make grants to Indian tribal governments or authorized designees of Indian tribal governments to—

(1) develop and enhance effective governmental strategies to curtail violent crimes against and increase the safety of Indian women consistent with tribal law and custom;

(2) increase tribal capacity to respond to domestic violence, dating violence, sexual assault, and stalking crimes against Indian women;

(3) strengthen tribal justice interventions including tribal law enforcement, prosecution, courts, probation, correctional facilities;

(4) enhance services to Indian women victimized by domestic violence, dating violence, sexual assault, and stalking;

(5) work in cooperation with the community to develop education and prevention strategies directed toward issues of domestic violence, dating violence, and stalking programs and to address the needs of children exposed to domestic violence;

(6) provide programs for supervised visitation and safe visitation exchange of children in situations involving domestic violence, sexual assault, or stalking committed by one parent against the other with appropriate security measures, policies, and procedures to protect the safety of victims and their children;

(7) provide transitional housing for victims of domestic violence, dating violence, sexual assault, or stalking, including rental or utilities payments assistance and assistance with related expenses such as security deposits and other costs incidental to relocation to transitional housing, and support services to enable a victim of

domestic violence, dating violence, sexual assault, or stalking to locate and secure permanent housing and integrate into a community; and

(8) provide legal assistance necessary to provide effective aid to victims of domestic violence, dating violence, stalking, or sexual assault who are seeking relief in legal matters arising as a consequence of that abuse or violence, at minimal or no cost to the victims.

(b) Collaboration—All applicants under this section shall demonstrate their proposal was developed in consultation with a nonprofit, nongovernmental Indian victim services program, including sexual assault and domestic violence victim services providers in the tribal or local community, or a nonprofit tribal domestic violence and sexual assault coalition to the extent that they exist. In the absence of such a demonstration, the applicant may meet the requirement of this subsection through consultation with women in the community to be served.

Under VAWA 2005, 7 percent from the Legal Assistance for Victims Improvements Program and 10 percent from the following six grant programs were combined to create the Grants to Indian Tribal Governments Program:

1. Grants to Combat Violent Crimes Against Women
2. Grants to Encourage State Policies and Enforcement of Protection Orders Program
3. Rural Domestic Violence and Child Abuse Enforcement Assistance Grants
4. Safe Havens for Children Program
5. Transitional Housing Assistance Grants for Child Victims of Domestic Violence, Stalking, or Sexual Assault Program
6. Court Training and Improvements Program.

VAWA 2013. §901. Grants to Indian Tribal Governments.

The VAWA 2013 amended the Grants to Indian Tribal Government Program by adding three new purpose areas that Indian tribes can use grant funds to support. These three purpose-areas reflect the concerns and recommendations made by tribal leaders during the annual consultation:

- Sex trafficking
- Services to address the needs of youth who are victims of domestic violence, dating violence, sexual assault, sex trafficking, or stalking, and the needs of youth and children exposed to domestic violence, dating violence, sexual assault, or stalking, including support for the non-abusing parent or the caretaker of the youth or child
- Development and promotion of legislation and policies that enhance best practices for responding to violent crimes against Indian women, including the crimes of domestic violence, dating violence, sexual assault, sex trafficking, and stalking.

Tribal Deputy in the Office on Violence Against Women VAWA 2005 §907

In 2005, Congress, recognizing the epidemic of violence against Native women and the complicated nature of implementing legal reforms and services in response to the violence, mandated that a position of Deputy Director for Tribal Affairs be created within the OVW. Congress enumerated clearly the duties and the authority of the Tribal Deputy Director within the statute. The importance of this position is illuminated in the context that the only statutorily created positions for OVW are that of the Director and the Deputy Director for Tribal Affairs.

Of all the provisions enacted under the Tribal Title of VAWA, the position of the Tribal Deputy Director is particularly important. The position is deemed essential for the successful implementation of the Tribal Title and VAWA provisions within tribal communities. It is designed as a central point of coordinating USDOJ responsibilities and programs to increase the safety of Native women, and supporting the efforts of Indian tribes.

The duties of the Tribal Deputy Director fall within four broad areas of responsibility mandated by statute:

1. Coordinate the ongoing intergovernmental activities required to conduct annual consultations with Indian tribes;
2. Serve as the point of coordination with various federal agencies and within the USDOJ on the implementation of the amended federal

statutes contained in VAWA 2005 by providing expertise in federal Indian law and policy;

3. Guide implementation of the research projects resulting from close coordination with the Research Task Force and direct the development of the tribal registries; and

4. Oversee administration of the Grants to Indian Tribal Governments Program and other tribal grants, contracts, and technical assistance programming.

Unfortunately, despite the statutory authority authorized by Congress in 2005, consistent understaffing of the tribal unit has significantly diminished the impact of the Tribal Deputy Director position. The complicated intersection of federal Indian law and tribal law requires the tribal unit be fully staffed to achieve successful implementation of VAWA in tribal communities. In 2013, Congress did not amend this section, although many tribal leaders at all past annual consultations have recommended that the staffing issue be addressed.

VAWA 2005. §907. Tribal Deputy in the Office on Violence Against Women.

(a) Establishment—There is established in the Office on Violence Against Women a Deputy Director for Tribal Affairs.

(b) Duties—

(1) In General—The Deputy Director shall under the guidance and authority of the Director of the Office on Violence Against Women—

(A) Grants. Contracts. Oversee and manage the administration of grants to and contracts with Indian tribes, tribal courts, tribal organizations, or tribal nonprofit organizations;

(B) ensure that, if a grant under this Act or a contract pursuant to such a grant is made to an organization to perform services that benefit more than one Indian tribe, the approval of each Indian tribe to be benefited shall be a prerequisite to the making of the grant or letting of the contract;

(C) coordinate development of federal policy, protocols, and guidelines on matters relating to violence against

Indian women;

(D) advise the Director of the Office on Violence Against Women concerning policies, legislation, implementation of laws, and other issues relating to violence against Indian women;

(E) represent the Office on Violence Against Women in the annual consultations under Section 903;

(F) provide technical assistance, coordination, and support to other offices and bureaus in the Department of Justice to develop policy and to enforce federal laws relating to violence against Indian women, including through litigation of civil and criminal actions relating to those laws;

(G) maintain a liaison with the judicial branches of federal, state, and tribal governments on matters relating to violence against Indian women;

(H) support enforcement of tribal protection orders and implementation of full faith and credit educational projects and comity agreements between Indian tribes and States; and

(I) ensure that adequate tribal technical assistance is made available to Indian tribes, tribal courts, tribal organizations, and tribal nonprofit organizations for all programs relating to violence against Indian women.

(c) Authority—

(1) In General—The Deputy Director shall ensure that a portion of the tribal set-aside funds from any grant awarded under this Act, the Violence Against Women Act of 1994 (Title IV of Public Law 103-322; 108 Stat. 1902), or the Violence Against Women Act of 2000 (division B of Public Law 106-386; 114 Stat. 1491) is used to enhance the capacity of Indian tribes to address the safety of Indian women.

(2) Accountability—The Deputy Director shall ensure that some portion of the tribal set-aside funds from any grant made under this part is used to hold offenders accountable through—

(A) enhancement of the response of Indian tribes to crimes of domestic violence, dating violence, sexual assault, and stalking against Indian women, including legal

services for victims and Indian-specific offender programs;
(B) development and maintenance of tribal domestic
violence shelters or programs for battered Indian women,
including sexual assault services, that are based upon the
unique circumstances of the Indian women to be served;
(C) development of tribal educational awareness programs
and materials;
(D) support for customary tribal activities to strengthen
the intolerance of an Indian tribe to violence against
Indian women; and
(E) development, implementation, and maintenance of
tribal electronic databases for tribal protection order
registries.

Firearms Possession Prohibition Expanded to Include Tribal Court Misdemeanor Convictions
VAWA 2005 §908(a)[84]

Gun control legislation in the United States has a long history, but it was not until the VAWA 2005 expanded the firearms possession prohibitions to include tribal law convictions that such legislation afforded enhanced protections for Native women. Congress passed the Federal Gun Control Act of 1968 (GCA) in part due to the assassinations of John F. Kennedy in 1963, and Senator Robert Kennedy and Dr. Martin Luther King in 1968. The GCA focused on restricting the purchase of handguns through the mail. It later restricted purchase of shotguns and rifles, and registration requirements.

In 1994, in the first authorization of the VAWA Congress amended the GCA to prohibit persons who are under a qualifying domestic violence court protection order from possessing or receiving a firearm.[85] "The dangerousness of guns and their adaptability [for] use in violent crime is why Congress has prohibited their possession by individuals subject to a domestic protection order . . . ."[86] Tribal court protection orders are included under this prohibited persons category. While Congress did not define the term "court order," it did provide the statutory requirements for prosecution under the amendment. It prohibits, subject to the commerce requirement, the shipping, transporting, receiving, or possessing of a firearm by any person:

(8) who is subject to a court order that—
(A) was issued after a hearing of which such person received actual notice, and at which such person had an opportunity to participate;
(B) restrains such person from harassing, stalking, or threatening an intimate partner of such person or child of such intimate partner or person, or engaging in other conduct that would place an intimate partner in reasonable fear of bodily injury to the partner or child; and
(C)(i) includes a finding that such person represents a credible threat to the physical safety of such intimate partner or child; or (ii) by its terms explicitly prohibits the use, attempted use, or threatened use of physical force against such intimate partner or child that would reasonably be expected to cause bodily injury.

The statutory requirements above apply to court orders restraining persons in the context of "intimate partners" or "child of such intimate partner." Court orders broader than the required "intimate partner" context would not meet the statutory requirement such as a court order in a non-intimate sexual assault or stalking case.

In 1996, Congress amended the GCA to include the Domestic Violence Offender Gun Ban [87] often referred to as the Lautenberg Amendment.[88] This amendment made it a federal felony for a person convicted of a qualifying misdemeanor crime of domestic violence to possess a firearm. This category of persons was added to the list of those prohibited under the GCA firearm prohibitions. GCA now bans shipment, transport, ownership, and use of guns or ammunition by individuals convicted[89] of qualifying misdemeanor domestic violence, or who are under a qualifying restraining order for domestic abuse. It is important to note, however, that the GCA does not include under its restrictions misdemeanor convictions of dating violence, sexual assault, and stalking. The Lautenberg Amendment represents the recognition by Congress that "anyone who attempts or threatens violence against a loved one has demonstrated that he or she poses an unacceptable risk, and should be prohibited from possessing firearms."[90]

The Lautenberg Amendment protections were eventually expanded under VAWA 2005 to include tribal court convictions of misdemeanor crimes of domestic violence, thus addressing a void involving protection of Native women. Section 908(a) expands the GCA by amending the federal criminal code to include under the term "misdemeanor crime of domestic violence" any offense that is a misdemeanor under tribal law. The amendment created a new federal offense that prohibits offenders convicted of a domestic violence crime in tribal court from possessing firearms. The tribal court conviction to qualify must meet the following statutory requirements of a misdemeanor crime of domestic violence under the GCA[91]:

> (33)(A) Except as provided in subparagraph (C), [FN2] the term "misdemeanor crime of domestic violence" means an offense that—
> (i) is a misdemeanor under federal, state, or tribal [FN3] law; and
> (ii) has, as an element, the use or attempted use of physical force[92], or the threatened use of a deadly weapon, committed by a current or former spouse, parent, or guardian of the victim, by a person with whom the victim shares a child in common, by a person who is cohabiting with or has cohabited with the victim as a spouse, parent, or guardian, or by a person similarly situated to a spouse, parent, or guardian of the victim
> (B)(i) A person shall not be considered to have been convicted of such an offense for purposes of this chapter, unless—
> (I) the person was represented by counsel in the case, or knowingly and intelligently waived the right to counsel in the case; and
> (II) in the case of a prosecution for an offense described in this paragraph for which a person was entitled to a jury trial in the jurisdiction in which the case was tried, either
> (aa) the case was tried by a jury, or
> (bb) the person knowingly and intelligently waived the right to have the case tried by a jury, by guilty plea or otherwise.
> (ii) A person shall not be considered to have been convicted of such an offense for purposes of this chapter if the conviction has been expunged or set aside, or is an offense for which the person has been pardoned or has had civil rights restored (if the law of the applicable jurisdiction provides for the loss of civil rights under such

an offense) unless the pardon, expungement, or restoration of civil rights expressly provides that the person may not ship, transport, possess, or receive firearms.

Under Section 908(a) it is a crime for a person convicted of domestic violence in tribal court or who is the subject of a protection order to transport, receive, or possess firearms or ammunition that have come across state or federal borders.

Firearms are extremely dangerous and lethal and pragmatic utilization of this statute has the potential to prevent serious injury to or murder of Native women. The Firearms Possession Prohibition is a federal law and thus only federal prosecutors or SAUSAs can charge perpetrators with this crime.[93] It is for this reason that training and coordination relative to Section 908(a) are essential for the successful implementation of this potentially lifesaving statute within Indian nations. Likewise, it is extremely important in locations where state-tribal concurrent jurisdiction exists that U.S. Attorneys are sufficiently trained and directed to be cognizant of this statute. This statute applies to firearm prohibitions committed on tribal lands within PL 280 or similar jurisdictions such as in Maine. The Bureau of Alcohol, Tobacco, Firearms and Explosives (ATF), an agency in the USDOJ, has primary investigative responsibility for the illegal use and trafficking of firearms.[94]

For Indian tribes, particularly justice personnel and advocates, it should be stressed that this federal crime most likely will not be charged unless gun violations are reported to the respective District United States Attorney. To initiate investigation and removal of weapons from a prohibited person or for assistance regarding firearms enforcement-related issues, contact should be made with the local ATF Office. In turn, the ATF will process a background check through the National Instant Criminal Background Check System, or NICS, on the person suspected of illegally possessing a firearm. NICS is located at the FBI's Criminal Justice Information Services Division in West Virginia. Entry of tribal convictions, particularly domestic violence convictions and orders of protection, into federal criminal databases, such as NICS, is essential to increasing the likelihood that firearms violations will be federally prosecuted under the GCA. Tribal efforts to establish a working relationship with the nearest offices of the U.S. Attorney and the ATF regarding enforcement of Section 908(a) will increase the likelihood of a swift response at the time of an emergency.

Intersection of Tribal Court Action, Federal Firearms Violation, and Federal Database

Tribal Court Action	Federal Firearms Violation	Federal Database
Conviction domestic violence maximum one year sentence (misdemeanor)	18 U.S.C. 922(g)(9)	NICS
Any conviction exceeding term of one year imprisonment (felony under TLOA)	18 U.S.C. 922(g)(1)	NICS
Domestic Violence Order of Protection	18 U.S.C. 922(g)(8)	NCIC Protection Order File and Triple I File[95]

In 2013, Congress did not amend this section and it remains as enacted in 2005.

VAWA 2005. §908(a). Firearms Possession Prohibition.

(a) Firearms Possession Prohibitions—Section 921(33)(A)(i) of Title 18, United States Code, is amended to read: "(i) is a misdemeanor under federal, state, or tribal law";

Misdemeanor Arrest Authority
VAWA 2005 §908(b)

Section 908(b) amends the Indian Law Enforcement Reform Act to provide misdemeanor arrest authority for federal officers and tribal specialized officers with reasonable grounds to believe that the person to be arrested has committed or is committing domestic violence, dating violence, stalking, or violation of a protection order and has as an element of the use or attempted use of physical force, or the threatened use of a deadly weapon.

VAWA 2005. §908(b). Misdemeanor Arrest Authority.

(b) Law Enforcement Authority—Section 4(3) of the
Indian Law Enforcement Reform Act, 25 U.S.C. §2803(3)
is amended—
(1) in subparagraph (A), by striking "or";
(2) in subparagraph (B), by striking the semicolon and
inserting ", or"; and
(3) by adding at the end the following:
"(C) the offense is a misdemeanor crime of domestic
violence, dating violence, stalking, or violation of a
protection order and has, as an element, the use or
attempted use of physical force, or the threatened use of a
deadly weapon, committed by a current or former spouse,
parent, or guardian of the victim, by a person with whom
the victim shares a child in common, by a person who is
cohabitating with or has cohabited with the victim as a
spouse, parent, or guardian, or by a person similarly
situated to a spouse, parent or guardian of the victim, and
the employee has reasonable grounds to believe that the
person to be arrested has committed, or is committing the
crime."

Domestic Assault by an Habitual Offender
VAWA 2005 §909

Domestic violence is a pattern of violence that escalates over time in severity and frequency. To prevent future violence and end the pattern, perpetrators must be held accountable immediately. Too often, habitual offenders are not identified.

The Violence Against Women Act of 2005 created the federal domestic violence crime, Domestic Assault by an Habitual Offender. It is a powerful charging tool that could make a tremendous difference for domestic violence victims as it grants the federal government jurisdiction over what otherwise would be deemed a misdemeanor offense.

VAWA 2005, Section 909[96] amended the federal criminal code to impose enhanced criminal penalties upon a repeat offender who: (1) commits a domestic assault within the special maritime and territorial jurisdiction of the United States or Indian country; and (2) has a final conviction on at least two separate prior occasions in federal, state, or tribal court for offenses that would be, if subject to federal jurisdiction, an assault, sexual abuse, or serious violent felony against a spouse or intimate partner, or a domestic violence offense.

Section 909 was intended to give federal prosecutors the authority to intervene in cases of repeated acts of domestic violence committed by tribal members that might not otherwise rise to the level of a felony. Cases can be prosecuted under this statute by the USDOJ in PL 280 and similar jurisdictions; therefore, it can be extremely useful when the state fails to prosecute domestic violence crimes committed on tribal lands.

Unfortunately, few cases are referred to the United States Attorneys' Offices for prosecution. One of the principal reasons for this lack of case referrals is that many tribal law enforcement officers or Bureau of Indian Affairs agents are unaware that an act of domestic violence committed on the reservation after two previous tribal convictions may be chargeable as a felony in federal court. Of particular importance to the charging of this statute are tribal court records of domestic violence convictions that are required to charge a defendant in federal court.

In an effort to increase the awareness of tribal law enforcement to potential federal prosecution options, USDOJ increased training and made available a training DVD. The DVD provides the applicable federal statues, evidence necessary to successfully prosecute a case in federal court, lethality assessments, safety planning, restitution, victim issues, and offender accountability.[97] Although utilization of this statue has not been maximized, the increased training on the statute has resulted in increased prosecutions.

In July 2011, the United States Court of Appeals for the Eighth and Tenth Circuits upheld the constitutionality of the statute. Both courts rejected a constitutional challenge to the use of uncounseled tribal court convictions as predicates for prosecution under the statute.[98] VAWA 2013 did not amend this section and the Habitual Offender statute continues to be an important prosecution option to hold offenders accountable for ongoing patterns of violence.

VAWA 2005. §909. Domestic Assault by an Habitual Offender.

(a) In General—Any person who commits a domestic assault within the special maritime and territorial jurisdiction of the United States or Indian country and who has a final conviction on at least two separate prior occasions in federal, state, or Indian tribal court proceedings for offenses that would be, if subject to federal jurisdiction—

(1) any assault, sexual abuse, or serious violent felony against a spouse or intimate partner; or

(2) an offense under chapter 110A, shall be fined under this title, imprisoned for a term of not more than 5 years, or both, except that if substantial bodily injury results from violation under this section, the offender shall be imprisoned for a term of not more than 10 years.

(b) Domestic Assault Defined—In this section, the term "domestic assault" means an assault committed by a current or former spouse, parent, child, or guardian of the victim, by a person with whom the victim shares a child in common, by a person who is cohabitating with or has cohabitated with the victim as a spouse, parent, child, or guardian, or by a person similarly situated to a spouse, parent, child, or guardian of the victim.

Grants to Indian Tribal Coalitions
VAWA 2013 §902

Early History—The 1970s

During the late 1970s and early '80s, American Indian and Alaska Native women opened their homes to help their sisters fleeing violence and seeking safety. This was during a time in the United States when violence against wives and girlfriends was not viewed as a serious problem. Referred to as "wife beating," domestic violence was rarely characterized as a violent crime even in the most severe cases.

While most Native women focused within their tribal communities as sisters helping sisters, some Native women joined their non-Native sisters within their respective states in the effort to organize a resistance to the violence. Native women like Roberta Crows Breast in North Dakota helped to found the North Dakota State Coalition, and Tillie Black Bear the South Dakota Coalition. In 1978, the National Coalition Against Domestic Violence (NCADV), composed of state coalitions and individual members from across the United States, was created.[99] The birth of the NCADV was due in part to the leadership of American Indian women survivors and advocates. Tillie Black Bear, a founding mother of NCADV, hosted the first meeting of the National Coalition in 1979 at the Rosebud Sioux Tribe's Reservation in South Dakota.

VAWA 2000 Establishment of Federal Funding for Tribal Coalitions

Since the late 1970s, the national movement for the safety of Native women has grown consistently, emerging initially from grassroots advocates based within tribal nations. This movement has in many ways upheld and advanced the right of Native women to live safely and free of violence. Over more than a decade (1977–1994), services have been established and laws passed enhancing protections from violence for tribal women. Over the passage of another five years (1995–2000), essential legal reforms were enacted into law, opening the door for the removal of institutionalized barriers preventing access to justice for Native women.

It has taken 30 years to establish the legal reforms contained in VAWA 2013 that provide the foundation to support the ongoing change needed in the everyday lives of Native women. Achieving full implementation of these and other needed reforms will take tremendous work over many years. Overall change occurs step-by-step over decades and lifetimes, as we have experienced and witnessed. A true blessing and strength of this movement has been the continuity in leadership that has maintained the steadfast voice of grassroots Native women nationally.

This tribal grassroots movement was largely unfunded given the lack of federal or state resources, and supported for the most part by advocates forming loose alliances to organize in resistance to the violence committed against women. While state coalitions[100] have received federal funding for over three decades, it wasn't until VAWA 2000 that tribal coalitions became eligible for federal funding.[101] At that time, it was recognized that tribal coalitions could, like their state coalition counterparts, provide training and education based on their tribal expertise to their tribal communities. This acknowledgment represented a tremendous step forward in that it opened the door for tribal coalitions to provide assistance based on the specific knowledge, practices, and beliefs it had of the communities requiring services.

VAWA 2013 Stabilization of Federal Funding

Today, 17 tribal coalitions[102] addressing sexual assault and domestic violence are recognized and funded by the Office on Violence Against

Women. These coalitions consist of members from tribal sexual assault and domestic violence programs, as well as individual women and men who are committed to ending the violence in their tribal communities and villages. The coalitions are regionally based and offer assistance that comes from their in-depth knowledge and understanding of the tribal communities within their respective service areas. The coalitions are an important information bridge in the development of state, federal, and tribal policies involving critical issues that impact the safety of women and the accountability of perpetrators. Tribal communities trust and rely on tribal coalitions to assist them with training and technical assistance essential to the provision of justice-related programs and victim services. While some state coalitions offer assistance to tribal communities, most do not have the requisite expertise in federal Indian law or laws of the respective Indian tribes, tribal organizations, or nonprofits to be served to provide meaningful, culturally appropriate technical assistance.

VAWA 2013 amended the tribal coalitions program to address stability issues and financial disparities between tribal and state coalitions. When the tribal coalition program was created under VAWA 2000, it was allocated 1/56th of the STOP program funding for support. At that time, only one tribal coalition existed in Wisconsin. With the growth of tribal coalitions from one at the start of the program in 2000 to seventeen in 2013, the funding allocation under the statute became inadequate. Unlike state coalitions that have separate dedicated federal funding streams for domestic and sexual assault programs, tribal coalitions have only one funding stream for both types of programs. Under the grant programs, each state coalition receives 1/56th of the funds available for each of its domestic and sexual assault programs. The disparity that exists is that all tribal coalitions together share 1/56th of allocated funds under the VAWA 2000 statute. This funding disparity remains an outstanding issue to be addressed.

While VAWA 2013 did not remedy the above disparity, it did increase the availability of funds for the tribal coalitions program by establishing a new funding set-aside. VAWA 2013 specifically created a new funding stream consisting of a 5 percent set-aside under the VAWA Grants to Encourage Arrest Program for the tribal coalitions program. The 2013 increase in funding will help make it possible for the tribal coalitions grant program to be administered on a formula basis, like the state coalition program. The VAWA 2013 amendment changing the tribal coalitions program from a competitive to a formula grant program increased the ability of each tribal program to utilize grant funds to meet the specific needs of their membership. It also eliminated expenses and staffing required to administratively manage separate grants. Additionally, the change from a competitive to a formula program reduced staff hours and cost associated with managing a competitive grant peer review process at the Office on Violence Against Women.

VAWA 2013 amendments to the tribal coalitions program are intended to bring stability by providing an increased funding level to be administered on an annual formula basis similar to the program for states and territories. The VAWA 2013 amendments addressed the following issues that hindered the development of the tribal coalitions by:

- Increasing stabilized funding for eligible, existing tribal coalitions;
- Providing available funding to support the development of future tribal coalitions in regions where none exist;
- Addressing the disparity between VAWA services for Native and non-Native women; and
- Providing critically needed and culturally appropriate technical assistance and training services for tribal communities by local and regional tribal experts.

Across the United States, tribal coalitions are organizing to inform and unite Indian nations and communities to increase the safety of Native women on a tribal and regional level through implementation of VAWA 2013.

A primary purpose of our tribal coalition is to provide training and technical assistance to Indian tribes in our region. Tribal leadership and programs responding to our women victimized by domestic violence or sexual assault are the critical links to implementing VAWA 2013. We must understand the tribal amendments of VAWA 2013 and develop a regional platform for action that fits the needs of our tribes and addresses the safety of Native women.

—Juana Majel Dixon,
Board President, Strong Hearted Native Women's Coalition
Southern Tribal Leaders 2013 VAWA Symposium,
Opening Session, September 18, 2013

VAWA 2013. §902. Grants to Indian Tribal Coalitions.

Section 2001 of Title I of the Omnibus Crime Control and Safe Streets Act of 1968 (42 U.S.C. 3796gg) is amended by striking subsection (d) and inserting the following:
(d) Tribal Coalition Grants—
(1) Purpose—The Attorney General shall award a grant to tribal coalitions for purposes of—
(A) increasing awareness of domestic violence and sexual assault against Indian women;
(B) enhancing the response to violence against Indian women at the federal, state, and tribal levels;
(C) identifying and providing technical assistance to coalition membership and tribal communities to enhance access to essential services to Indian women victimized by domestic and sexual violence, including sex trafficking; and
(D) assisting Indian tribes in developing and promoting state, local, and tribal legislation and policies that enhance best practices for responding to violent crimes against Indian women, including the crimes of domestic violence, dating violence, sexual assault, sex trafficking, and stalking.
(2) Grants—The Attorney General shall award grants on an annual basis under paragraph (1) to—
(A) each tribal coalition that—
(i) meets the criteria of a tribal coalition under section 40002(a) of the Violence Against Women Act of 1994 (42 U.S.C. 13925(a));
(ii) is recognized by the Office on Violence Against Women; and
(iii) provides services to Indian tribes; and
(B) organizations that propose to incorporate and operate a tribal coalition in areas where Indian tribes are located but no tribal coalition exists.
(3) Use of Amounts—For each of fiscal years 2014 through 2018, of the amounts appropriated to carry out this subsection—
(A) not more than 10 percent shall be made available to organizations described in paragraph (2)(B), provided that 1 or more organizations determined by the Attorney General to be qualified apply;

(B) not less than 90 percent shall be made available to tribal coalitions described in paragraph (2)(A), which amounts shall be distributed equally among each eligible tribal coalition for the applicable fiscal year.

(4) Eligibility for Other Grants—Receipt of an award under this subsection by a tribal coalition shall not preclude the tribal coalition from receiving additional grants under this title to carry out the purposes described in paragraph (1).

(5) Multiple Purpose Applications   Nothing in this subsection prohibits any tribal coalition or organization described in paragraph (2) from applying for funding to address sexual assault or domestic violence needs in the same application.

Tribal Jurisdiction Over Non-Indians in Crimes of Domestic Violence
VAWA 2013 §904

Faced with these criminal and civil jurisdictional limitations, tribal leaders repeatedly have told the Department that a tribe's ability to protect a woman from violent crime should not depend on her husband's or boyfriend's race, and that it is immoral for an Indian woman to be left vulnerable to violence and abuse simply because the man she married, the man she lives with, the man who fathered her children, is not an Indian.

—Thomas Perrelli,
Associate Attorney General, USDOJ
Statement, Senate Committee on Indian Affairs on July 14, 2011

In 2013, VAWA was reauthorized to amend the Indian Civil Rights Act in specific cases of non-Indians abusing Native women on land under the jurisdiction of an Indian tribe. This amendment was intended to close the jurisdictional loophole that prevented Indian tribes from prosecuting non-Indian abusers committing domestic violence, dating violence, or violating an order of protection.

During the debates prior to the reauthorization of VAWA 2013, the reality that non-Indian abusers commit domestic violence against Native women within tribal jurisdiction and typically faced no criminal consequences was undisputed. Through numerous Congressional hearing and briefings, the dangerous truth became clear that Indian tribes did not have the authority to prosecute such offenders and the federal and, in some cases, state and local entities were far away from the scene of the crime. It became further evident that such federal, state, and local entities also did not have the resources to prosecute these cases and, in some instances, did not have the will.

The devastating impact of this jurisdictional loophole on the daily lives of Native women seeking safety from a non-Indian abuser is understood most graphically through the stories of Native women who survived such abuse. During the efforts by the NCAI Task Force to inform Congress of the need to close the gap in the law, Native women who had experienced the consequences of Indian tribes not having the prosecutorial authority to hold domestic abusers accountable stepped forward to tell their stories.

Diane Millich traveled to Washington, DC, to participate in a briefing sponsored by the House Native American Caucus and share her story and how the amendment to restore jurisdiction over non-Indian abusers could save the lives of Native women. Billie Jo Rich, after attending a community meeting during which her tribal councilwoman presented on the opposition to the tribal jurisdiction amendment in Congress, wrote the letter below in which she courageously tells the story of her non-Indian abuser. Billie Jo shared her ordeal and the impact of her tribe not having authority over her non-Indian husband upon her safety and that of her children.

Statement of Diane Millich

House Briefing
The Violence Against Women Reauthorization Act and
Safety for Indian Women
Canon House Office Building – Room 402
Thursday, May 10, 2012, 10:30 a.m.–12:00 p.m.

Good Morning,

Early yesterday morning I drove from my home to Durango and flew to DC in the hope that my story will help to explain why it is urgent that Indian tribes have jurisdiction over non-Indian abusers living and working on tribal land.

I have been diagnosed with lupus and will begin chemotherapy in just a few days on May 12. I have a serious illness and want you to know this so it will help you appreciate and understand just how important Sections 904 and 905 are to me and thousands of other Native women.

When I was 26 years old, I lived on my reservation and started dating a non-Indian, a white man. I was in love and life was wonderful. After the bliss of dating for six months we were married.

To my shock, just days after our marriage he assaulted me. I left and returned over 20 times. After a year of abuse and more than 100 incidents of being slapped, kicked, punched, and living in horrific terror, I left for good. During that year of marriage, I lived in constant fear of attack. I called many times for help, but no one could help me.

I called the Southern Ute tribal police, but the law prevented them from arresting and prosecuting my husband. Why? They could not help me because he was a non-Indian—because he was white. We lived on the reservation, but tribal police have no authority over a non-Indian. I called the La Plata County deputy sheriff, but they could not help me because I was a Native woman living on tribal land.

All the times I called and tribal police came and left only made my ex-husband believe he was above the law. All the times the county deputy sheriffs came and left only made him believe he could beat me and that he was untouchable. My reporting of the violence only made it worse.

I called so many times, but over the months not a single arrest was made. On one occasion after a beating, my ex-husband called the county sheriff himself to show me that no one could stop him. He was right; two deputies came and confirmed they did not have jurisdiction. I was alone and terrified for my safety.

Section 904 would have allowed tribal law enforcement to have arrested my abuser and stopped the violence being committed against me. It will allow an Indian tribe that meets all of the requirements of the statute to arrest and prosecute a non-Indian who lives or works on an Indian tribe's land and commits misdemeanor domestic violence or violates an order of protection.

My story would have been different if Section 904 had been the law at the time.

Instead, the violence that started with slapping and pushing escalated over the months. All the signals he received were green lights to continue his violence and destruction of my home, property, and my life. The brutality increased after I left and filed for a divorce and the order of protection.

I felt like I was walking on eggshells and knew inside that something terrible was going to happen. I was at home and he pulled up to my house. I ran and got in my car while he tried to break the windows. After I fled, he broke into the house breaking windows, furniture, and dishes. He cut the knuckles of his hands during the violence and smeared his blood over the walls, the floor, and my bedroom sheets. My home was destroyed.

The next day, I was at work and saw him pull up in a red truck. I was so afraid that something terrible was going to happen. My ex-husband told me, "You promised until death due us part so death it shall be." He was armed with a 9mm gun.

If not for my very brave coworker I would not be alive today. My coworker prevented my murder by pushing me out of harm and unfortunately took the bullet in his shoulder.

The shooting took place at a federal Bureau of Land Management land site where we both worked. The jurisdictional issue is so complicated that after the shooting investigators used a measuring tape at the scene to determine jurisdiction, the point where the gun was fired from and where the bullet landed. It took hours just to decide who had jurisdiction over the shooting.

The nightmare only continued after the shooting because he fled the scene and was not apprehended until two weeks later in New Mexico and arrested on drug and weapons offenses. I stayed at a shelter from time of the shooting until the arrest.

The U.S. Attorney and District Attorney agreed the District would prosecute the case. Because he had never been arrested or charged for any of the domestic violence crimes against me on tribal land, the District treated him as a first-time offender. They offered him a plea agreement.

The District Attorney offered a plea of aggravated driving under revocation. He took it immediately. In the end, none of the domestic violence or the shooting incident were charged. It was like his attempt to shoot me and the shooting of my coworker did not happen.

The tribe wanted to help me and would have charged the domestic violence crimes but could not because of the law. In the end, he was right in that he was above the law.

I also could not receive victim compensation to help with the destruction to my home, car, and property because the violence was committed on tribal land and the case prosecuted by the District Attorney.

I also want to share with you why Section 905 is also so important to Native women who are victims of domestic violence and dating violence.

We need help and are told that an order of protection will prevent future violence. Although the Southern Ute Indian tribe could not prosecute my husband, the tribal court did grant me an order of protection. The tribal court and I both believed the order of protection would help keep me safe—that it would prevent future violence.

Unfortunately, my abuser believed he was above tribal law. He did not consider the tribal order valid and laughed at it. His abuse increased after I was granted the order. It increased also after the county refused to enforce the order.

Section 905 will clarify that a tribal court does have the authority to issue orders of protection over all persons and also enforce the order.

The message to my ex-husband was clear—that his violence against me as an American Indian woman living on my tribal land has no legal consequence. The legal system following the law failed me.

I want everyone here today to know that American Indian women do not have the same protections as non-Indian women. Federal law, as you have heard from my story, has a large, gaping hole in it for abusers who are non-Indian. It is important that you understand that this is about race in America today.

If I were white, my story would be different. If I lived off of tribal land, my story would be different. I am a Native woman, and my family has lived on our reservation for over seven generations. These are facts that will not change.

Please speak for us.

Thank you.
Diane Millich

Letter from Billie Jo Rich to Eastern Band of Cherokee Indians Councilwoman Terri Henry

14 February 2013
Dear Councilwoman Terri Henry,

When I was in my early twenties, I found myself going through a nasty divorce from my non-enrolled husband. (I am enrolled.) During the course of our marriage, he hit me once "accidentally" when he became angry during a play pillow fight. But the violence became more of a theme in the months leading up to our court date for the divorce.

During that time, I had left the home we shared in both our names (but on land, in my name only, of course) because I had been told by the police that they could not make him leave. I felt I had to leave since the only alternative was to reside there with him. I ended up spending most of that year with my mother in her tiny singlewide trailer. My children remained in their home with their father, and I brought them to my mother's tiny trailer for visitations.

My ex-husband, whom we will call "J" for the sake of this narrative, seemed unwilling to ever bring the children to me in any public place, preferring to have me come and get them from our house. I hated to do that more than anything because it always seemed to result in some type of altercation. During one of these, the police were called. While we stood outside talking to the officers, J made a remark about putting me into the river. While the police didn't comment or even seem to notice the remark, it chilled me. What they didn't know, and J knew all too well, was that not only can I not swim, but I am actually terrified of deep water. J's comment was a veiled threat to end my life. In fear, I pointed this out to the officers who still pretended they didn't hear anything. When I pointedly told them that J had just threatened me, and made them admit they had heard it, they seemed very embarrassed. They both just looked at the ground and quietly told me they couldn't do anything about it.

There were many instances like this, but one in particular is still difficult to think about. One sunny afternoon in May, I was returning my daughters to their father per our agreement. I dropped them off and made sure he was home and they were in the house before leaving as usual, but their father walked out to stand beside my car. Cautious, I stayed in the car with the door locked, but car windows were down. He seemed agreeable enough at first, but then became angry because I did not wish him a happy anniversary. I quietly stated that it didn't seem appropriate under the circumstances. He suddenly lunged in the car window and snatched my bag, removing a small address book. He flipped through it and became angry, then suddenly lunged in again and snatched my car keys from the ignition and walked away. I jumped out of the car and began struggling with him to get the car keys back. I panicked, knowing I had no other keys and I really needed to get away from there. He held the keys high above his head as he walked away, drew back his hand as if to throw the keys out into the woods, and I jumped up and down beside him trying to reach them. J is well over six feet tall and I am about five foot five.

When it became apparent I wasn't going to get my keys back, I turned to walk away. He then threw the keys to the ground. When I leaned over to get them, he kicked me, and when I fell across the ground he kicked me again, causing me to roll down a small embankment to where my car was parked. My younger daughter, who was around three or four at that time, happened to be standing beside my car. As I rolled down the hill, I cut her feet out from under her and she fell. Since I was already on the ground, I pulled her into my arms to comfort her. Immediately, J loomed over us. He grabbed her arms and pulled her so hard that even though he was not touching me directly, I was dragged across the ground. So of course, I let go of her. I didn't want to hurt her. The minute I let go, J threw her into his car and sped away.

Once I got my car keys, I left also and went straight to the police department. But that's where he had gone as well. He beat me there, and had told them that I had knocked my daughter down and that I was a danger to my children. He was granted a protective order for himself and both my daughters. He told them he was afraid I would hurt my children. And I sat in that police department in torn clothing, with grass and leaves on my clothes and in my hair. I had a bruise forming on my side that would develop into an almost-perfect footprint from where he had kicked me, and the police told me there was nothing they could do because J was not enrolled.

One time, he grabbed my hand and twisted it up behind my back, flinging me to the floor on my knees with my face shoved into the couch. He jammed his knee into my back so hard I thought I would pass out. I heard a snapping sound, which I thought at the time was one of my artificial fingernails breaking. When I finally got away from him I was surprised to see that none of my fingernails were broken. The next day, as I was helping my mother load flats of bedding plants onto her truck, I bumped my hand. It

103

hurt so bad I saw stars. When I went to the ER to get my hand checked, an X-ray showed a broken bone in my finger. That was the snapping sound I had heard. There was no swelling, but the bone was broken. I knew better than to go to the police at this point. I knew there was nothing they could do to help me. I truly believed, and I think he did too, that he could kill me and they would do nothing.

Thankfully, he did not kill me, and I am safely away from him for good.

And so, almost 20 years later, I feel compelled to speak about my experiences because my tribal council representative gave some information at a community meeting about the VAWA. I was stunned that after all these years I still had an emotional reaction, and things I hadn't thought about in a long time bubbled up to the surface. It was difficult and surprisingly still painful to remember and, in a way, relive my experiences. But the emotion I feel now is relief, because hopefully these provisions will allow Native women to finally feel safe from their attackers, enrolled or non-enrolled. Native women no longer have to feel afraid or helpless.

Thank you, Terri. Words cannot express my gratitude.
Billie Jo Rich

Tribal Domestic Violence Criminal Jurisdiction:
Three Specific Crimes Covered

For thirty-five years, since 1978, Indian tribes did not have criminal jurisdiction over domestic violence and dating violence crimes committed by non-Indians in Indian country. Passage of the "special domestic violence criminal jurisdiction" statute specifically provided tribes with criminal jurisdiction to prosecute non-Indians committing these same crimes. This amendment simply eliminates the race of the offender from the equation. Congress by inclusion of this amendment were of the mind that race should not play a role in bringing an offender to justice, and in bringing justice to a victim.

The amendment was narrowly tailored to cover three specific crimes commonly committed by non-Indians threatening the safety of Native women and stability of Indian communities. The three crimes enumerated and defined in this section are:

- Domestic violence
- Dating violence
- Violations of protection orders

The basis for proving the elements of the crime would be the laws of the Indian tribe prosecuting the case.

Non-Indian abusers must have "sufficient ties to the Indian tribe."

This jurisdictional amendment is narrowly crafted to hold non-Indian offenders accountable and does not provide broad tribal jurisdiction over all persons or all types of crimes. To assume the proposed "special domestic violence criminal jurisdiction," the statute requires that a tribe show that any non-Indian defendant being prosecuted has sufficient ties to the Indian tribe. To establish "sufficient ties," a tribe is required to prove the non-Indian defendant has at least one of the following ties:

- Resides in the Indian country of the prosecuting tribe,
- Is employed in the Indian country of the prosecuting tribe, or
- Is the spouse, intimate partner, or dating partner of a member of the prosecuting tribe or an Indian residing in the Indian country of the prosecuting tribe.

The section allows an Indian tribe to assume "special domestic violence jurisdiction" over non-Indian abusers who live, work, and/or maintain intimate relationships in Indian country. It is intended to prevent non-Indians from violating tribal laws with impunity just because of their non-tribal member status. It further recognizes that it is in the interest of public safety to hold violent abusers accountable for crimes of domestic violence at the early stage before their acts of violence escalate.

Constitutional safeguards are required.

The section requires Indian tribes to guarantee Indian and non-Indian defendants the same constitutional rights to counsel that would be available in federal or state court. It also requires that an Indian tribe exercising such jurisdiction comply with two other federal statutes.

First, it requires that an Indian tribe provide non-Indian defendants all protected rights as provided by the Indian Civil Rights Act. In 1968, Congress enacted the Indian Civil Rights Act that protects individual liberties and constrains the powers of tribal governments in much the same ways that the Federal Constitution limits the powers of the federal and state governments. The Indian Civil Rights Act protects numerous rights for defendants in tribal court, including the following rights, among others:

- The right against unreasonable search and seizures.
- The right not to be twice put in jeopardy for the same offense.
- The right not to be compelled to testify against oneself in a criminal case.
- The right to a speedy and public trial.
- The right to be informed of the nature and cause of the accusation in a criminal case.
- The right to be confronted with adverse witnesses.
- The right to compulsory process for obtaining witnesses in one's favor.
- The right to have the assistance of defense counsel, at one's own expense.
- The rights against excessive bail, excessive fines, and cruel and unusual punishments.
- The right to the equal protection of the tribe's laws.
- The right not to be deprived of liberty or property without due process of law.
- The right to a trial by jury of not less than six persons when accused of an offense punishable by imprisonment.
- The right to petition a federal court for habeas corpus, to challenge the legality of one's detention by the tribe.

Second, the section requires that an Indian tribe provide non-Indian defendants the same rights afforded Indian defendants under the Tribal Law and Order Act of 2010. In 2010, Congress passed the Tribal Law and Order Act, which (among other things) amended the Indian Civil Rights Act to allow tribal courts to impose longer sentences. In return, the 2010 amendments require tribal courts imposing longer sentences to undertake additional measures to safeguard defendants' rights. The legislation applies these additional safeguards to domestic violence cases with shorter sentences, as well. These rights include:

- The right to effective assistance of counsel at least equal to that guaranteed by the United States Constitution.
- The right of an indigent defendant to the assistance of a licensed defense attorney at the tribe's expense.
- The right to be tried by a judge with sufficient legal training who is licensed to practice law.
- The right to access the tribe's criminal laws, rules of evidence, and rules of criminal procedure.
- The right to an audio or other recording of the trial proceeding and a record of other criminal proceedings.

Any opposition to tribal special domestic violence jurisdiction over non-Indians is unfounded since Indian tribes are required to provide licensed defense counsel to non-Indian defendants who cannot afford to hire counsel. Indian tribes must meet this requirement in any criminal proceeding where imprisonment is possible.

—Juana Majel Dixon,
First Vice President,
National Congress of American Indians

Clarification of Tribal Orders of Protection
VAWA 2013 §905

VAWA 2013 confirms the intent of Congress in enacting the Violence Against Women Act of 2000 by clarifying that every tribe has full civil jurisdiction to issue and enforce certain protection orders involving any persons, Indian or non-Indian. "Two key Senate committees prepared reports that address the specific language eventually adopted as Section 905 of VAWA 2013. Both reports reflect Congress' intent that Section 905 clarify and confirm the existing authority of all tribes to issue and enforce protective orders against anyone, Indian or non-Indian, for matters arising in Indian country of the Indian tribe or otherwise within the authority of the tribe."[103] The section effectively reverses *Martinez* v. *Martinez*,[104] which held that an Indian tribe lacked authority to enter a protection order for a non-member Indian against a non-Indian residing on non-Indian fee land within the reservation.

The Martinez Case

Daniel and Helen Martinez lived on non-Indian fee-owned land within the reservation boundaries of the Suquamish Tribe. Helen Martinez and their children are members of the Alaska Native Village of Savoonga. Between 2007 and 2008, both parties filed and utilized tribal court on domestic matters involving protection orders, child custody, visitation, and divorce.

The Court raised many eyebrows in the logic of its ruling. "The Court does not construe the provisions of the VAWA as a grant of jurisdiction to the Suquamish Tribe to enter domestic violence protection orders as between two non-members of the tribe who reside on fee land within the reservation. There is nothing in this language that explicitly confers upon the tribal jurisdiction to regulate non-tribal member domestic relations. The grant of jurisdiction simply provides jurisdiction 'in matters arising within the authority of the tribe.'"

The Suquamish Tribal Code specifically provides that any person may petition the tribal court for an order of protection by filing a petition alleging he or she has been the victim of domestic violence committed by the respondent.[105] However the Court's position is that "There must exist 'express authorization' by federal statute of tribal jurisdiction over the conduct of non-members (p. 6). For there to be an express delegation of jurisdiction over non-members, there must be a 'clear statement' of express delegation of jurisdiction."

A concern amongst many tribal experts and practitioners existed that confusion from the Martinez case might cause many victims of domestic and sexual violence seeking a protection order from a tribal court to question whether such an order would increase their safety. Orders of protection are a strong tool to prevent future violence but are only as strong as the recognition and enforcement provided by other jurisdiction of such an order.

VAWA 2013 amended Section 2265 of Title 18, United States Code, by striking subsection (e) and inserting the following:

> (e) Tribal Court Jurisdiction.—For purposes of this section, a court of an Indian tribe shall have full civil

jurisdiction to issue and enforce protection orders involving any person, including the authority to enforce any orders through civil contempt proceedings, to exclude violators from Indian land, and to use other appropriate mechanisms, in matters arising anywhere in the Indian country of the Indian tribe (as defined in Section 1151) or otherwise within the authority of the Indian tribe.

Amendments to the Federal Assault Statute
VAWA 2013 §906

The VAWA Amendments of 2013 bring the federal criminal code into the 21st century.

—John Harte, Mapetsi Policy Group

Beginning in the 1980s, a cultural shift brought about the recognition that wife battering was not a private affair within the four walls of a home. With the education of criminal justice personnel by the movement for battered women, state laws were passed making domestic violence a crime. Within many states, the belief that a husband had the absolute right to discipline his wife and children was replaced with recognition that domestic violence is a public safety issue. The door started to close on a time when police were trained to mediate "domestic disputes," and prosecutors were told not to file these "no-win" cases.

Unfortunately, federal criminal law had not developed over time to provide the same protection for Native women. While the devastating consequences of domestic violence against Native women and tribal communities are no less compelling, the federal assault statutes had not provided the same response over the last three decades. VAWA 2013 amended the federal criminal code to make sentencing options more consistent with state laws. It is hoped that the impact of these amendments will ensure that abusers acting on Indian lands will be subject to similar potential punishments.

Appropriate Penalties to Signal Domestic Violence Is a Serious Crime

Penalties often signal to offenders and societies the seriousness of the crime. Previously, federal law subjected non-Indian offenders who abused

Native women on Indian lands to no more than a potential six-month misdemeanor for assault or assault-and-battery offenses. However, few federal prosecutors have the time or resources to handle many misdemeanor cases. In 2006, U.S. Attorneys prosecuted only 24 misdemeanor cases arising in Indian country, and only 21 in 2007.

A federal prosecutor typically can charge a felony offense against an Indian or a non-Indian defendant only when the victim's injuries rise to the level of "serious bodily injury," which may require life-threatening injury or permanent disfigurement. As a result, in assaults that involved strangling or suffocating, substantial (but not serious) bodily injury, and striking, beating, or wounding, federal prosecutors often could not seek sentences in excess of six months. When such misdemeanor cases committed by non-Indians go unprosecuted, the victim and the tribal community have nowhere to turn for justice. The offenders become emboldened and the level of violence increases in their attacks.

VAWA 2013 addresses this problem by increasing the maximum sentence from six months to one year for an assault by striking, beating, or wounding. Although the federal offense remains a misdemeanor, increasing the maximum sentence to one year reflects the reality that this is a serious offense that often forms the first or second rung on a ladder to more severe acts of domestic violence.

Assaults resulting in substantial bodily injury sometimes form the next several rungs on the ladder of escalating domestic violence, but they too were inadequately covered by the federal criminal code. VAWA 2013 filled this gap by amending the code to provide a five-year offense for assault resulting in substantial bodily injury to a spouse, intimate partner, or dating partner.

In addition, VAWA 2013 amends the code to provide a 10-year offense for assaulting a spouse, intimate partner, or dating partner by strangling or suffocating. Strangling and suffocating—conduct that is not uncommon in intimate partner cases—carry a high risk of death. But the severity of these offenses is frequently overlooked because there may be no visible external injuries on the victim. As with assaults resulting in substantial bodily injury, federal prosecutors needed the tools to deal with these crimes as felonies, with sentences potentially far exceeding the six-month maximum that previously existed.

Lastly, the amendments to the federal assault statutes amends the Major Crimes Act to cover all felony assaults under Section 113 of the federal criminal code that include the two new felony offenses discussed above—assaults resulting in substantial bodily injury to a spouse, intimate partner, or dating partner; and assaults upon a spouse, intimate partner, or dating partner by strangling or suffocating—as well as assault with intent to commit a felony other than murder, which is punishable by a maximum 10-year sentence.

These outdated federal statutes represented just a few of the many systemic barriers separating Native women from all other women in the United States. These amendments, taken together, have the potential to greatly improve the safety of women in tribal communities. They equip federal and tribal law enforcement agencies, working in partnership, with appropriate legal consequences to hold all domestic violence abusers accountable for their crimes.

Effective Dates and Pilot Project for Tribes Implementing Tribal Jurisdiction Over Non-Indians
VAWA 2013 §908

The passage of VAWA 2013 opened the door for Indian tribes to protect Native women abused by non-Indians within the jurisdiction of certain Indian tribes. Implementations of these important amendments to the Indian Civil Rights Act are underway. Section 908 of VAWA 2013 details the effective dates of the tribal amendments and a pilot project period.

Effective Dates

With respect to Special Domestic Violence Criminal Jurisdiction (SDVCJ) over non-Indians, the effective date is March 7, 2015 (two years after the date of enactment on March 7, 2013). At any time during the two-year period beginning on the date of enactment, an Indian tribe may ask the Attorney General to designate the tribe as a participating tribe to exercise SDVCJ on an accelerated basis. Under this section, the Attorney General can approve a tribe earlier than March 7, 2015, to exercise such jurisdiction during the pilot project phase.[106] The statute provides that the Attorney General may grant such a request after coordinating with the Secretary of the Interior, consulting with affected Indian tribes, and concluding that the criminal justice system of the requesting tribe has adequate safeguards in place to protect defendants' rights, consistent with the section.

Pilot Project Phase

The Department of Justice in implementing Section 908 developed two phases for the pilot project period. Phase One is a planning and assessment phase, which began in the spring of 2013 and is ongoing. Phase Two is the implementation phase, which started in late 2013 and will run through March 7, 2015. In Phase Two, a tribe seeking approval to exercise SDVCJ must complete and submit an application questionnaire promulgated by USDOJ and attach relevant excerpts of the tribe's laws, rules, and policies. This application questionnaire is the mechanism by which tribes formally request to be designated as a participating tribe and seek approval from the Attorney General to implement SDVCJ on an accelerated basis. The Final Notice was published in the Federal Register on November 29, 2013.[107]

On February 6, 2014, the USDOJ announced its first round of approvals of tribes who applied to implement SDVCJ under the Pilot Project. The three tribes are (in alphabetical order): the Confederated Tribes of the Umatilla Indian Reservation (Oregon); the Pascua Yaqui Tribe (Arizona); and the Tulalip Tribes (Washington). Under the VAWA Pilot Project, these tribes will be able to exercise criminal jurisdiction over certain crimes of domestic violence and dating violence, regardless of the defendant's Indian or non-Indian status, beginning February 20, 2014.

Since the effective date, each tribe has continuously engaged efforts to develop training to update law enforcement officers as well as court personnel, to examine codes and procedures for any necessary amendments to clarify the scope of its SDVCJ authority, and to develop applicable forms, procedures, and orders. Each of the tribes has a Special Assistant United States Attorney to increase the likelihood that every viable violent offense against Native women is prosecuted in either federal court or tribal court, or both. All three tribes have made several arrests of non-Indian alleged domestic violence offenders; cases are under investigation and set for trial.

Intertribal Technical Assistance Working Group

To assist interested Indian tribes in the process of implementation of SDVCJ over non-Indians and granting approval of request by tribes to begin exercising such jurisdiction prior to March 7, 2015, during the pilot period, the USDOJ launched the Intertribal Technical Assistance Working Group (ITWG) in June of 2013. The ITWG is essentially a collaborative work group composed of tribal officials, justice experts, and USDOJ personnel working together to develop best practices on combating domestic violence and criminal procedures necessary to successfully implement SDVCJ. Currently, 39 tribes have representatives participating in the ITWG.

Intertribal Technical Assistance
Working Group on Special Domestic Violence
Criminal Jurisdiction (ITWG)

1. Cherokee Nation
2. Chickasaw Nation
3. Colorado River Indian Tribes of the Colorado River Indian Reservation
4. Confederated Tribes of the Umatilla Indian Reservation
5. Eastern Band of Cherokee Indians
6. Eastern Shawnee Tribe of Oklahoma
7. Gila River Indian Community of the Gila River Indian Reservation
8. Fort Peck Assiniboine & Sioux Tribes
9. Hopi Tribe of Arizona
10. Kickapoo Tribe of Oklahoma
11. Menominee Tribe of Wisconsin
12. Mississippi Band of Choctaw Indians
13. Muscogee (Creek) Nation
14. Nez Perce Tribe
15. Nottawaseppi Huron Band of the Potawatomi
16. Oneida Tribe of Indians of Wisconsin
17. Pascua Yaqui Tribe of Arizona
18. Passamaquoddy Tribe
19. Pauma Band of Mission Indians
20. Penobscot Indian Nation
21. Pokagon Band of Potawatomi Indians
22. Prairie Band Potawatomi Nation
23. Pueblo of Isleta
24. Pueblo of Laguna
25. Pueblo of Santa Clara
26. Quapaw Tribe
27. Quinault Indian Nation
28. Sac and Fox Nation
29. Salt River Pima-Maricopa Indian Community

30. Sault Ste. Marie Tribe of Chippewa Indians
31. Seminole Nation of Oklahoma
32. Sisseton-Wahpeton Oyate of the Lake Traverse Reservation
33. Spokane Tribe
34. Standing Rock Sioux Tribe of North and South Dakota
35. Suquamish Indian Tribe of the Port Madison Reservation
36. Three Affiliated Tribes of the Fort Berthold Reservation
37. Tulalip Tribes of Washington
38. White Earth Nation
39. Winnebago Tribe of Nebraska

Extension of the Indian Law and Order Commission VAWA 2013 §909

The Tribal Law and Order Act (TLOA), signed into law by President Obama in July 2010 with bipartisan support, provides greater freedom for tribes to design and run their own criminal justice systems. The TLOA created the Indian Law and Order Commission (ILOC), an independent advisory group to help with the greatest challenges to securing equal justice for Native Americans living and working on Indian lands.

The ILOC was required by the TLOA to submit a report to the President and Congress with recommendations intended to make Native American and Alaska Native nations safer and more just for all U.S. citizens and to reduce the unacceptably high rates of violent crime that have plagued Indian country for decades.

> When Congress and the Administration ask why the crime rate is so high in Indian country, they need look no further than the archaic system in place, in which federal and state authority displaces tribal authority and often makes tribal law enforcement meaningless.
>
> —ILOC Report

The VAWA 2013 extended the ILOC from two years to three years, until January 2014, to submit its report and recommendations on the continuation of the Alaska Rural Justice and Law Enforcement Commission.

The ILOC Report, titled "A Roadmap for Making Native America Safer,"[108] was submitted to the President and Congress in November 2013.

The report reflects one of the most comprehensive assessments ever undertaken of criminal justice systems servicing Native American and Alaska Native communities. The Senate Committee conducted an oversight hearing on the report on February 12, 2014.

Section 909. Indian Law and Order Commission Report on the Alaska Rural Justice and Law Enforcement Commission

(a) In General.—Section 15(f) of the Indian Law Enforcement Reform Act (25 U.S.C. 2812(f)) is amended by striking "2 years" and inserting "3 years".
(b) Report.—The Attorney General, in consultation with the Attorney General of the State of Alaska, the Commissioner of Public Safety of the State of Alaska, the Alaska Federation of Natives, and federally recognized Indian tribes in the State of Alaska, shall report to Congress not later than one year after enactment of this Act with respect to whether the Alaska Rural Justice and Law Enforcement Commission established under Section 112(a)(1) of the Consolidated Appropriations Act, 2004, should be continued and appropriations authorized for the continued work of the commission. The report may contain recommendations for legislation with respect to the scope of work and composition of the commission.

Special Rule for the State of Alaska – Repealed December 18, 2014 VAWA 2013 §910

As originally enacted, Sections 904 and 905 of the Violence Against Women Reauthorization Act of 2013 applied to only one of 229 Alaska Native Villages. Under VAWA 2013 Section 910. Special Rule for the State of Alaska, special domestic violence criminal jurisdiction applied only to the Metlakatla Indian Community, Annette Island Reserve, and excluded all other tribes in Alaska. Section 904 recognizes and affirms inherent jurisdiction of federally recognized tribes to prosecute non-Indians who violate orders of protection or commit domestic or dating violence against Indian victims on tribal lands.[109] Section 905 clarifies tribal jurisdiction to issue and enforce orders of protection over all persons.[110]

However, on December 18, 2014, President Obama signed into law a repeal of Section 910. The legislation passed by the 113th Congress contains one sentence that effectively strikes the Alaska exemption from VAWA 2013. It states simply, "Section 910 of the Violence Against Women Reauthorization Act of 2013 is repealed."[111]

Lenora Hootch, Co-Chair, NCAI Task Force on Violence Against Women, commented, "I'm really excited. We'll be able to provide safety and jurisdiction to our tribes in our state. I want to thank all those who supported us and worked hard to repeal the section. The government needs to give back our sovereign rights. All the issues we face in the villages, those belong to us. They cannot keep coming to the villages and saying they can fix things for us because they don't know our way of life. We know the resources and because we live among each other we know how to help our own people. I strongly believe that if we have full authority the healing process will begin."

Senator Murkowski explained that her support for Section 910 as an amendment under VAWA 2013 was based on her understanding that the provision restoring criminal jurisdiction to Indian tribes over certain non-Indian perpetrators in domestic violence cases was not intended for Alaska tribes: "VAWA never was designed or intended to expand the powers of Alaska tribes over non-members of a tribe."[112] Despite staunch opposition by the Alaska Federation of Natives, Alaska tribal leaders and advocates, the NCAI Task Force on Violence Against Women, and the National Task Force to End Violence Against Women, Section 910 was enacted in VAWA 2013.

Inclusion of Section 910 created an outcry across Alaska Native Villages[113] and Indian tribes within the lower forty-eight states.[114] During the 2013 and 2014 VAWA consultations held by the Department of Justice, Alaska Native leaders presented oral statements[115] and others submitted written testimony calling for its repeal.[116] This tribal call to action was strengthened by support from numerous national non-tribal organizations, the White House[117], and the U.S. Department of Justice.[118] This groundswell led, in part, to the Alaska Congressional delegation's successful efforts toward repealing Section 910.

Following the repeal of Section 910, the Alaska Congressional delegation remarked, in a joint press release, on the importance of the repeal.[119] Senator Murkowski stated: "Alaska tribes asked me to repeal Section 910 of VAWA and I heard them loud and clear." Representative Don Young stated, "In the many conversations I have had with the Alaska Native leaders and families since the reauthorization of VAWA last year, I heard a consistent, clear, and powerful message that Section 910 was an error and must be repealed."

Although Alaska Natives represent only 15.2 percent of the state population, they comprise nearly 50 percent of domestic violence victims, and 61 percent of sexual assault victims.[120] Like their Native sisters in the lower forty-eight states, Alaska Native women in their villages and across the state experience violence at epidemic rates. Alaska Native Villages, hindered by a jurisdictional maze similar to the one that confronts Indian tribes elsewhere in the United States, face additional barriers resulting from federal law and Supreme Court rulings specific to Alaska.

"The inconsistent recognition of tribal authority, coupled with the poor response from state law enforcement, has created an extremely dangerous environment for Alaska Native women," said Tamra Truett Jerue, Tribal Administrator for the Native Village of Anvik, and member of the Alaska Native Women's Resource Center. Many advocates, like Truett Jerue, recognize that violence against Native women occurs as a spectrum in the lives of American Indian and Alaska Native women and understand that the violence is undeniably linked to the steady erosion of tribal sovereign authority to protect women.

These laws, policies, and practices have created an environment in which Alaska Native women are particularly vulnerable to the five crimes of domestic violence, sexual assault, dating violence, stalking, and sex trafficking, all of which are included within the Safety for Indian Women Title of VAWA 2013. Dr. David Lisak,[121] a national expert on perpetrators of sexual assault, who has provided training for the Office on Violence Against Women on the pattern of sexual predators, has often remarked, "Predators attack the unprotected. The failure to prosecute sex crimes against American Indian women is an invitation to prey with impunity." Likewise, the following testimony excerpt provided at the Indian Law and Order Commission hearing describes the desperate need to address this epidemic:

> Every woman you've met today has been raped. All of us. I know they won't believe that in the lower forty-eight, and the state will deny it, but it's true. We all know each other and we live here. We know what's happened. Please tell Congress and President Obama before it's too late.[122]

The Indian Law and Order Commission (ILOC), established under the Tribal Law and Order Act of 2010, studied Alaska and made recommendations to Congress and President Obama on what can and should be done to restore enhanced authority to Alaska Native Villages.[123] The ILOC findings and recommendations provide a fuller context to the importance of the repeal of Section 910. The opening paragraph to the chapter titled "Reforming Justice for Alaska Natives: The Time Is Now" reads:

> Section 205 of the Tribal Law and Order Act of 2010 (TLOA) states, *"Nothing in this Act limits, alters, expands, or diminishes the civil or criminal jurisdiction of the State of Alaska, any subdivision of the state of Alaska, or any Indian tribe in that state."* Yet, the Indian Law and Order Commission's opinion is that problems in Alaska are so severe and the number of Alaska Native communities affected so large that continuing to exempt the state from national policy change is wrong. It sets Alaska apart from the progress that has become possible in the rest of Indian country. The public safety issues in Alaska—and the law and policy at the root of those problems—beg to be addressed. These are no longer just Alaska's issues. They are national issues.

Repeal of Section 910 was a necessary step to provide Alaska Native Villages the authority to enhance their response to violence against Native women who suffer the highest rates of domestic and sexual violence in the nation. However, as most supporters of the repeal acknowledge, additional reforms are required to increase safety for Alaska Native women and hold offenders accountable. Also, while the Alaska exemption was recently repealed, Section 904's limitation that criminal jurisdiction extends to only crimes committed in "Indian country" continues to effectively deny 228 of 229 federally recognized Alaska tribes of new protections afforded other Indian tribes because of the Supreme Court's holding in *Alaska v. Native Village of Venetie*.[124] However, this may change in the near future in light of a recent ruling that will allow the Department of Interior to accept land into trust for all federally recognized Alaska Native tribes. This marks an historic change in federal policy. The regulation was developed after the U.S. District for the District of Columbia ruled in *Akiachak Native Community v. Salazar*[125] that the exclusion of Alaska tribes from the land-into-trust process was unlawful. Placing Alaska Native lands into trust will make them subject to federal criminal laws protecting Native women, and will allow Alaska tribes to exercise local tribal governance to address the public safety crises facing Alaska Native women.

VAWA 2013. §910. Special Rule for the State of Alaska – Repealed December 18, 2014

(a) Expanded jurisdiction

In the State of Alaska, the amendments made by Sections 904 and 905 shall only apply to the Indian country (as defined in Section 1151 of Title 18, United States Code) of the Metlakatla Indian Community, Annette Island Reserve.

(b) Retained jurisdiction

The jurisdiction and authority of each Indian tribe in the State of Alaska under Section 2265(e) of Title 18, United States Code (as in effect on the day before the date of enactment of this Act)—

(1) shall remain in full force and effect; and

(2) are not limited or diminished by this Act or any amendment made by this Act.

(c) Savings provision

Nothing in this Act or an amendment made by this Act limits or diminishes the jurisdiction of the State of Alaska, any subdivision of the State of Alaska, or any Indian tribe in the State of Alaska.

Chapter 4 Notes

[68] Violence Against Women and Department of Justice Reauthorization Act of 2005, Public Law 109-162, as amended by Public Law 109-271.
[69] Violence Against Women Act, Title IV of the Violent Crime Control and Law Enforcement Act of 1994 (Public Law 103-322).
[70] Division B of the Victims of Trafficking and Violence Prevention Act of 2000, Public Law 106-386.
[71] Public Law 109-162, as amended by Public Law 109-271.
[72] Public Law 113-114
[73] *Supra note* 1, Title IX. Safety for Indian Women.
[74] Executive Order 13175, Consultation and Coordination with Indian Tribal Governments (November 6, 2000).
http://www.gpo.gov/fdsys/pkg/FR-2000-11-09/pdf/00-29003.pdf.
[75] Published at 74 Fed. Reg. 57879 (November 9, 2009, and available at http://www.gpo.gov/fdsys/pkg/DCPD- 200900887/pdf/DCPD-200900887.pdf.
[76] U.S. Department of Justice, Office on Violence Against Women Tribal Consultation Reports:

> 2013 report:
> http://www.justice.gov/sites/default/files/pages/attachments/2014/08/15/2013ovw-tc-report.pdf.
> 2012 report:
> http://www.justice.gov/sites/default/files/ovw/legacy/2013/06/05/2012ovw-tc-report.pdf.
> 2011 report:
> http://www.justice.gov/sites/default/files/ovw/legacy/2012/11/28/2011-tribal-consultation-report.pdf.
> 2010 report:
> http://www.justice.gov/sites/default/files/ovw/legacy/2012/10/25/2010-tribal-consultation-report.pdf.
> 2009 report:
> http://www.justice.gov/sites/default/files/ovw/legacy/2012/11/28/2009-tribal-consultation-report.pdf.

[77] Members of the 2008 Task Force included: Jacqueline Agtuca, Director of Public Policy, Clan Star, Inc., Cherokee, NC; Cheryl Neskahi Coan, Director of Training and Technical Assistance, Southwest Indigenous Women's Coalition, Phoenix, AZ; Jolanda Ingram, Director, Niwhongwh Xw E Na Wh Stop the Violence Coalition, Hoopa Valley, CA; Pamela Iron, Executive Director, National Indian Women's Health Resource Center, Tulsa, OK; Hon. Billy Jo Jones, Director, Northern Plains Tribal Judicial Training Institute, Chief Judge, Sisseton-Wahpeton Tribe, Rapid City, SD; Lori Jump, Program Manager, Advocacy Resource Center, Sault Ste. Marie Tribe of Chippewa Indians Victim Services Program, Sault Ste. Marie, MI;

Bernadette LaSarte, Program Director, Coeur d'Alene Tribal Domestic Violence Program, Plummer, ID; Patricia McGeshick, Program Director, Ft. Peck Family Violence Resource Center, Poplar, MT; Denise Morris, President, Alaska Native Justice Center, Inc., Anchorage, AK; Arlen Quetawki, Zuni Pueblo Law Enforcement Consultant, Pueblo of Zuni, NM; Hon. Vikki Shirley, First Lady, Navajo Nation, Window Rock, AZ; and Nancy J. Soctomah, Project Coordinator, Peaceful Relations Domestic Violence Response Program, Pleasant Point Reservation, ME.

[78] Recommendations on the National Institute of Justice Proposed Program of Research Under the VAWA 2005, Safety for Indian Women Title, Section 904 (March 18, 2010). Available at http://www.justice.gov/ovw/section-904-task-force.

[79] Reauthorization of the Violence Against Women Act of 2005, Title IX, §905(a).

[80] Tribal Law and Order Act of 2010, Pub. L. No. 111-211, Title II, 124 Stat. 2279, §233(b)(1), 28 U.S.C. §534(d).

[81] http://www.justice.gov/ovw/2013-tribal-consultation#docs.

[82] http://www.gpo.gov/fdsys/pkg/PLAW-111publ211/pdf/PLAW-111publ211.pdf.

[83] http://www.hsgac.senate.gov/download/?id=d77a8cba-fc3c-440d-966e-30cb06b36ee6.

[84] Reauthorization of the Violence Against Women Act of 2005, Title IX, § 908(a).

[85] 18 U.S.C. §922(g)(8).

[86] United States v. Rogers, 371 F.3d 1225, 1229 (10th Cir. 2004).

[87] 18 U.S.C. §922(g)(9).

[88] Named after its sponsor, Senator Frank Lautenberg (D-NJ).

[89] 18 U.S.C. §921(a)(33)(B)(ii).

[90] Congressional Record, p. S1187, September 30, 1996.

[91] 18 USC 921(33)(B)(i).

[92] *United States v. Castleman*, 572 U.S. ___ (2014), slip opinion 12-1371, Opinion of the Court, Sotomayor, J., March 26, 2014. "Congress incorporated the common-law meaning of 'force'—namely offensive touching—in §921(a)(33)(A)'s definition of a misdemeanor crime of domestic violence." Note: Under *Castleman* review of a tribal or state definition of a crime of "domestic violence" is timely in the context of *Castleman*; particularly, in the prosecution of a non-Indian offender under VAWA 2013 special domestic violence jurisdiction. See for example the definition of domestic violence of the Tulalip Tribes Code, Title 4 Youth, Elders and Family, Chapter 4.25. http://www.codepublishing.com/wa/Tulalip.

[93] http://www.justice.gov/usao/eousa/foia_reading_room/usam/title9/crm01117.htm.

[94] http://www.atf.gov/content/firearms.

[95] The NCIC Triple I file contains misdemeanor crimes of domestic violence.

[96] 18 U.S.C. §117.

[97] *Using Federal Law to Prosecute Domestic Violence Crimes in Indian Country.* Available at http://www.ovc.gov/pdftxt/DVIC_facilitator_guide.pdf.

[98] See *United States v. Cavanaugh,* 643 F.3d 592 (8th Circuit, 2011) and *United States v. Shavanaux,* 647 F.3d 993 (10th Circuit, 2011).

[99] http://www.ncadv.org.

[100] Funding to territorial coalitions was amended in VAWA 2005 to address inequities between coalitions located within states and those located within the territories.

[101] Victims of Trafficking and Violence Protection Act of 2000, Division D = Violence Against Women Act of 2000, Public Law No. 106-386. 114 Stat. 1496, §1103, (c)(3)(4). ("(4) 1/54 shall be available for the development and operation of nonprofit tribal domestic violence and sexual assault coalitions in Indian country"). http://www.gpo.gov/fdsys/pkg/PLAW-106publ386/html/PLAW-106publ386.htm.

[102] USDOJ, Office on Violence Against Women, FY 2013 Tribal Domestic Violence and Sexual Assault Coalitions Program Solicitation, expired June 30, 2013, p. 3. http://www.justice.gov/sites/default/files/ovw/legacy/2013/04/15/fy2013-tribal-coalitions-solicitation.pdf.

[103] Memorandum on Legislative History of Section 905 of VAWA 2013 (Indian Law Resource Center 2015), available at http://www.indianlaw.org/sites/default/files/Sec_905_Leg_History.

[104] *Martinez v. Martinez,* 2008 WL 5262793, No. C08-55-3 FDB (W.D. Wash. Dec. 16, 2008).

[105] Suquamish Tribal Code §7.28.2.

[106] http://www.justice.gov/tribal/docs/wava-tribal-pilot-project-faqs.pdf.

[107] https://www.federalregister.gov/articles/2013/11/29/2013-28653/pilot-project-for-tribal-jurisdiction-over-crimes-of-domestic-violence.

[108] The UCLA American Indian Studies Center serves as the sole repository for the Indian Law and Order Commission's materials: http://aisc.ucla.edu/iloc.

[109] 25 U.S.C. 1304.

[110] 18 U.S.C. 2265(e).

[111] Alaska Safe Families and Villages Act of 2014, Pub. L. 113-275.

[112] Senator Lisa Murkowski, *Op-Ed: Ending abuse, securing justice in Alaska* (March 31, 2013), http://www.murkowski.senate.gov/public/index.cfm/2013/3/op-ed-ending-abuse-securing-justice-in-alaska.

[113] Alaska Federation of Natives, Inc., 2013 Annual Convention, *Protect Alaska Native Women, Resolution 13-14* (October 26, 2013), http://www.nativefederation.org/publications/resolutions.

[114] National Congress of American Indians, *Protect Alaska Native Women*, #REN-13-006 (June 2013), http://www.ncai.org/resources/resolutions/protect-alaska-native-women.

[115] Alaska Native leaders included: Mike Williams, Chief of the Yupiit Nation Consortium of Federally Recognized Tribes, and Chairperson Mary Ann Mills, Kenaitze Indian Tribe, Kenai, Alaska.

[116] Lenora Hootch, Tribal Council, Village of Emmonak, Violence Against Women Act Annual 2013 Consultation (November 14, 2013); Carl Jerue, Chief, Anvik Tribe, VAWA 2013 Annual Consultation written testimony (January 7, 2014); Donald Adams, Chief/President, Tetlin Village, written testimony of Tetlin Tribal Council for 2013 USDOJ Tribal Consultation (January 10, 2014); and Michael Williams, Native Village of Akiak, 2013 Annual VAWA Consultation (January 14, 2014). In addition, two organizations comprised of Indian tribes submitted written testimony: the Alaska Federation of Natives and the National Congress of American Indians. USDOJ, Office on Violence Against Women, *2013 Tribal Consultation Report* (June 2014), http://www.justice.gov/sites/default/files/pages/attachments/2014/08/15/2013 ovw-tc-report.pdf.

[117] Vice President Joseph Biden, *Remarks White House Tribal Nations Conference* (December 4, 2014), http://www.c-span.org/video/?323039-1/white-house-tribal-nations-conference.

[118] Tony West, Associate Attorney General Tony West Speaks at the Attorney General's Advisory Committee on American Indian and Alaska Native Children Exposed to Violence Hearing, Justice News (June 11, 2014), http://www.justice.gov/opa/speech/associate-attorney-tony-west-speaks-attorney-general-s-advisory-committee-american-indian.

[119] Lisa Murkowski, Don Young, *Duo's Efforts Solidified Support to Remove Provision as Congress Adjourns* (December 12, 2014), http://www.murkowski.senate.gov/public/index.cfm/2014/12/murkowski-young-assure-vawa-amendment-repeal.

[120] UAA Justice Center Report to the Council on Domestic Violence and Sexual Assault (May 13, 2010).

[121] David Lisak, Ph.D., forensic consultant, professional trainer, and lecturer at the University of Massachusetts, Boston, http://www.davidlisak.com.

[122] Tribal citizen (name withheld) statement provided during an Indian Law and Order Commission site visit to Galena, Oklahoma, October 18, 2012.

[123] Indian Law and Order Commission, *A Roadmap For Making Native America Safer, Report to the President and Congress of the United States* (2013), http://www.aisc.ucla.edu/iloc/report/files/Chapter_2_Alaska.pdf.

[124] *Alaska v. Native Village of Venetie Tribal Government*, 522 U.S. 520 (1998).

[125] *Akiachak Native Community v. Salazar*, 935 F. Supp. 2d 195 (D.D.C. 2013).

Chapter 5

Stronger Together: VAWA—A National Platform for Organizing to Remove Outstanding Barriers to the Safety of Native Women

The National Congress of American Indians (NCAI) Task Force has served as the umbrella organization through which the grassroots movement effectively reauthorized VAWA in 2005 and 2013. The challenge for the Task Force and grassroots movement looking forward is to continue to provide clear direction on a national agenda for change. The process of developing such an agenda will be aided by understanding the movement building that has taken place since 2003.

The victories achieved through the reauthorization of VAWA 2005 and 2013 were the result of a national platform developed by the Task Force. The targeted reforms contained in VAWA 2005 and 2013 discussed in previous chapters originated from grassroots advocates and tribal women's coalitions. [126] Representatives of tribal women's coalitions drafted resolutions identifying and addressing these issues and presented them to NCAI membership for a vote during national meetings. Adoption of these resolutions by NCAI—as the oldest and largest member organization of Indian tribes in the United States—represented the strongest statement of a national platform to enhance the safety of Native women.

To continue to achieve such national reforms, the movement is again challenged to identify the fundamental barriers to the safety of Native women on a national level and offer solutions to remove such barriers. Many of the barriers are woven into federal laws and policies created decades ago during the Termination Era. These barriers serve as the foundation of the violence that impact Indian tribes and tribal communities across the United States, and solutions for removing the barriers are needed on a national level. As we have experienced from the 2005 and 2013

VAWA reauthorizations, the platform is not stagnant but changes over time as gains are made nationally.

Changing national law and policies is no small task, and the greater the change the larger the groundswell that is needed. The development of a platform of unity must be broad enough to build a national movement. In this sense, it must represent and unite a cross section of actual stakeholders linked to the safety of Native women. During the 2005 and 2013 VAWA reauthorizations, this included primarily Indian tribes, tribal coalitions, and grassroots advocates.

On a national level, the day-to-day leadership of NCAI was essential.[127] On local and regional levels, tribal organizations, such as the United South and Eastern Tribes, the Great Plains Chairmen's Association, and the All Indian Pueblo Council, were critical points of contact for senators and members of Congress. In June 2012, when it seemed VAWA would not be reauthorized due to opposition to the tribal jurisdictional amendments, elected tribal women leaders stepped forward to lobby Congress. Alongside these leaders stood Native women who suffered the violence of non-Indians. Standing stronger together, these women walked the halls of Congress and as representatives of their tribal nations served as a catalyst for the 2013 victory.[128]

Indian women and advocates for their safety have and will continue to be the actual heart of the national movement. Since the late 1970s, these women have worked to build local and regional responses to the violence in the form of safe houses and shelters. As VAWA resources became available in the late 1990s to fund full-time advocacy programs, these efforts began to grow into a national network. With the creation of a national tribal coalition program under VAWA 2000 to support regional education and organizing of tribal advocacy providers, a national focus developed. While not all coalitions are actively involved in the effort to inform national change, many are rooted in an understanding of the negative linkage between safety of Native women and federal laws and policies.

Like the layers of an onion, the movement must peel away layer upon layer of federal laws and policies that have made Native women the most vulnerable population of women in the United States. Predators prey upon the vulnerable, and the lack of justice services, poverty, stigmatization, lack of access to healthcare services, and often rural isolation are rooted in historic periods culturally dominated by arrogance and hatred of Native peoples. The epidemic rates of violence against Native women are an extension of colonization. Although peeling back the layers and understanding the path to remove these barriers and create solutions remain as complicated as ever, the movement operating under the NCAI umbrella is larger than ever before.[129] Through the process of organizing the tribal grassroots movement to accomplish these gains, the Task Force has summarized important lessons in understanding this path forward. These lessons can serve as guiding lights for our movement in the years to come.

For many years the Indian Law Resource Center took on the responsibility for raising the struggles of American Indian Nations on an international level. In 2010, Terri Henry and Jacqueline Agtuca attended the United Nations Periodic Review of the human rights record of the United States in Geneva, Switzerland. At that time, they learned of Rashida Manjoo's plan to visit the United States, and invited her to include Native women in her itinerary and to visit Qualla Boundary,[130] the home of the Eastern Band of Cherokee Indians. In preparing for the visit, the planning committee was challenged to summarize and explain the barriers to and the solutions for the safety of Native women to an international audience. In addition, following Ms. Manjoo's visit, the NCAI Task Force leadership retreated to discuss the direction forward.[131] In this way, the visit of the Special Rapporteur challenged the Task Force to summarize the barriers and recommendations for legal reform—a national platform for change— to an international audience.[132] The Task Force also summarized lessons learned from organizing efforts over the years, which are discussed below.

Native Women Facing Danger Without Services

The progress made since 1995 although substantial must be understood in the context of the extent of the epidemic of violence and also the lack of resources available to assist Native women. One of the guiding principles identified is the reality that a large population of Native women face life-threatening violence on a daily basis and need immediate assistance. This population of Native women is waiting for access to justice. As Tillie Black Bear said during the retreat to prepare for Ms. Manjoo's visit, "Native women cannot wait for the system to be fixed. They need help now to stay alive and stop the violence of their abusers."

Understanding that the reform of government systems to respond to such violence is ongoing and may take decades, it was clear that Native women could not wait. The Task Force needed to address this reality by considering the following questions: How will this reform increase services for Native women? What about the women? How will services for Native women be included through national reform? It was the hope that answering such questions could provide clarity.

The words of Tania, an advocate and Native woman, is a voice for the population of Native women waiting to be served. Statistics cannot count this population and research cannot reveal the depth of the suffering endured by Native women and their nations.

As I sat in the courtroom yesterday for my jury duty for a rape case, the prosecutor questioned all potential jurors, a standard process. The prosecutor asked whether anyone had been a victim of a similar crime and felt they would be too adversely impacted by personal experience to be able to listen to the testimony or give a fair verdict. Two women of the pool of nearly 40 raised their hands and were excused. Later he asked if anyone had had a close friend or family member who was victimized in such a way; about a half dozen had, one of whom was excused.

Later on, he asked flat out if any in the jury pool had been a victim of rape. Slowly, about 10 hands were raised. Apparently several others, like myself, had experienced rape but didn't feel compelled to respond to the earlier question because we didn't feel so adversely affected as to render us incapable of being effective jurors. As horrific as the incident was, we all had become "comfortable" with our story, as it was such a normal part of us. The impact of our victimization may have been diminished by time, therapy, denial, or survival skills such as selective memory, and we sat there in broad daylight and claimed that we were not too impacted by our experiences. As the prosecutor went juror by juror, asking details of when the rape occurred, whether it had been reported, prosecuted, in what court it had been charged (if any) and if there was a conviction, and how we felt about the results and the judicial system, we all gave our stories. Brief as they were, we sounded like AA meeting participants where instead of giving our names we gave our juror badge numbers and stated our anonymous facts: "Number 21. I was raped 'x' number of years ago, and it was never reported or prosecuted."

After each one finished their testimony, the prosecutor asked, "Any more?" and more hands would raise. By the time he ran out of jurors to call on, instead of the 10 who initially responded with hands raised, nearly every hand had risen and all but about 3 women and the 3 men present had told of their experience. I wondered how many of those who spoke had ever admitted out loud what had happened to them before. I was sure some never had. Oh the power and courage breaking the silence inspires!

How tragic it was that this random sampling of our community showed about a 90 percent rate of women reporting they had been raped, especially when we know so many won't openly admit it for *any* reason, no matter if they are under oath, because of denial, fear, guilt, shame, or other reasons; so the sampling of that room could easily have been 100 percent in actuality! And how ironic of us all introducing ourselves as numbers when we are the very statistics we talk about on a regular basis and the act of rape dehumanizes us and makes us a case number if we report and a majority number if we don't.

For my experiences and strong opinions I was quickly excused from the jury selection, and while I claimed non-impact by my history, I left the courtroom heavily impacted by what I had just witnessed, knowing it wasn't a rare freak coincidence but it is actually the reality we live in. With tears I was rejuvenated and committed to make a difference, even if the slightest of one, in hopes that one day the reality will be different and that our sisters, daughters, and mothers will be safe!

—Tania, CCT Advisory Committee Against Domestic Violence[133]

Support for the Safety of Alaska Native Women and Sovereignty of Alaska Native Villages

In the struggle to increase the safety of Native women nationally, the NCAI Task Force has recognized the urgent nature and complex legal barriers to enhancing the safety of Alaska Native women. While violence against Native women has reached epidemic levels on tribal lands, the rates of violence against Alaska Native women are even greater. Alaska Native women are subjected to the highest rate of forcible sexual assault in the country.[134] One in two Alaska Native women will experience sexual or physical violence, and "an Alaska Native woman is sexually assaulted every

18 hours."[135] This human rights crisis is linked to the current justice system that leaves Alaska Native women without adequate and in many cases any legal protection.

> The greatest legal barriers to the safety of Native women have been created by federal laws and policies that stripped the authority of our village to respond to domestic and sexual violence. We were then denied the resources to create a village-based justice system to keep our village safe. Local control is the alternative to a broken system that has not worked.

> Currently, when a crime occurs in which a woman is being beaten, the village responds to that cry for help, because she is our community member. As her relative and community member, we must stand with her. It is our responsibility, but this is a dangerous situation for the woman and for those protecting her and stopping the violence. Our village is the local government and it acts to protect our members. Recognizing this reality in all of our villages and restoring the legal authority of villages to respond to crimes and make decisions regarding the safety, health, and well-being of residents is an essential next step in addressing the issues of domestic violence, sexual assault, suicide, and substance abuse/alcohol-related deaths.[136]

> —Tami Truett Jerue, Alaska Native Village of Anvik
> June 2014

The crisis confronting Alaska Native women within villages requires a national response and the efforts of the NCAI Task Force to achieve national reforms to increase the safety of Native women must highlight this need for immediate change. The sovereignty of all Indian nations is linked and the safety of all Native women requires that Alaska Native women not be left behind. In discussions of a national platform for increasing the safety of Native women, the national movement must rally to support inclusion of the reforms needed for Alaska Native women to live free of violence within their villages.[137] Further, the sovereignty of Alaska Native Villages to protect women must be supported to enhance accountability of perpetrators within the villages.

Alaska has one of the highest per-capita rates of physical and sexual abuse in the United States. While Alaska Natives comprise 15.2 percent of the population in Alaska, nearly 50 percent of the victims of domestic violence and 61 percent of the victims of sexual assault are Alaska Natives.[138] According to one regional study, Native women in the Ahtna region are three times more likely to experience domestic violence than other women in the United States, and 8 to 12 times more likely to experience physical assault.[139] The statistics were even worse among Athabascan women, 64 percent of whom reported that they had experienced domestic violence.[140] Approximately half of the perpetrators in these situations are also Alaska Native.

> —Julie Kitka, President, Alaska Federation of Natives;
> Wade Henderson, President, Leadership
> Conference on Civil and Human Rights;
> and Nancy Zirkin, Vice President,
> Leadership Conference on Civil and Human Rights,
> in a May 7, 2012, letter to Congressman Don Young

Of the 229 Alaska Native Villages, 165 are off-road communities that are only accessible by air for most of the year. Ninety of these 165 off-road communities also do not have any form of law enforcement. Alaska tribes fall within four state judicial districts and 229 tribal jurisdictions. Tribal and state jurisdiction overlap as Public Law 280 created concurrent, shared jurisdiction between the state and Alaska Native Villages. The result of this concurrent jurisdiction has created ongoing confusion as to who is ultimately responsible for responding to incidents of violent crime within a village. Since the enactment of PL 280 in the early 1950s, jurisdictional confusion has created numerous roadblocks for the safety of Native women.

To many involved with the state judicial system, PL 280 was interpreted to mean that the state was in charge of responding to these incidents. This state interpretation, however, was in contrast to the fact that PL 280 did not alter tribal jurisdiction but only transferred limited federal jurisdiction to certain states. The U.S. Supreme Court decision in *Alaska v. Native Village of Venetie Tribal Government*[141] created even greater confusion in ruling that very limited Indian country exists in Alaska.

While these jurisdictional issues are being resolved, the reality is that the 229 village governments that existed prior to PL 280 continue to exist following PL 280. These village governments are most often the only real authority available for hundreds of air miles to assist a woman in the face of or following a violent attack. These villages have existed for hundreds of years and safeguarded the lives of their women based on the unwritten laws embedded within their cultures, languages, and beliefs. The village of Tetlin is one of the many villages with a strong response to domestic violence and sexual assault.

Tetlin Village is a traditional village, originated by the Athabascan people traveling seasonally between fishing and hunting camps. The village is located on the Tetlin River, approximately 20 miles away from Tok Junction between the Tanana River and Tetlin Lake, and has a population of about 370 members. Tetlin is the only village in the Tok area, which does not only rely on a haul road system; access is by boat, snow machine, or airplane depending on climatic conditions.

Tetlin Village has a fully functioning tribal court, which focuses on problem solving and strategic planning within the community to prevent crime and violence. The tribal court has made every effort to work with the Alaska State Troopers and state court systems. Today, this system between the tribes and the State of Alaska is not working to track offenders/perpetrators to protect our victims. We have invited the state courts to work with us relating to the tracking system, but this has not been established as a priority by the State of Alaska as a collaborative effort despite our repeated efforts to reach out to the state.

Furthermore, Tetlin Village has a written code of tribal ordinances and is a product of many minds and many hours of work. Through the knowledge gained from listening to our grandparents and elders, these individuals were able to construct this code, which reflects the traditional values of the Tetlin people. Moreover, as a result of our combined and thoughtful efforts to address issues within Tetlin, our tribal court is a competent and strong court system, which is better structured than distant state courts to handle local prosecutions. The Tetlin Tribal Court currently handles domestic violence and sexual assault cases. As such, the tribal court hears cases and can provide an order of protection, dissolve or modify an order of protection, and oversee protection order violations. Our tribal court orders are stamped with a Tetlin Tribal Court Stamp.[142]

—Nettie Warbelow, Alaska Village of Tetlin
June 2014

Looking forward, the national movement must address the epidemic levels of violence committed against Alaska Native women by expansion of VAWA to reach Alaska Native women living within their villages. Such reform should recognize that local jurisdiction is the proper solution to create such safety. Not only are Alaska Native Villages federally recognized Indian tribes, they are also often the only government for hundreds of air miles. Unfortunately, the response of state justice personnel is often inadequate and in some instances nonexistent. When and if a report of an act of violence against a woman or child is made, it can take the Alaska state troopers anywhere from one to ten days to respond. In some cases, it may take longer depending upon weather conditions, the urgency of the other matters they are dealing with in other villages, the apparent severity of the situation, and so forth. If they do respond, it is commonly after the period for mandatory arrest of the perpetrator in domestic violence cases or after the 72 hours recommended for a sexual assault forensic examination.

These circumstances create the dangerous reality that frequently the only people standing between a woman in need of protection from a batterer or rapist are family or local community members. In many instances, this role falls upon a local domestic violence advocate. Consequently, the life of a woman depends largely on the local community's ability to provide immediate assistance.

In November 2013, the Indian Law and Order Commission (ILOC or Commission) released its findings and recommendations in a report, *A Roadmap for Making Native America Safer*. The report, released by a nine-member volunteer commission, and which took over two years to compile, presented 40 bold recommendations that provide stirring possibilities for Indian tribes to pursue in order to ensure public safety within their respective communities. With respect to Alaska, the Commission's findings served as a call for critical and urgent action to improve public safety—once again reemphasizing support for local control. The unanimous view of the Commission found that the "problems in Alaska are so severe and so large, that continuing to exempt the state from national policy change is wrong [and that] the public safety issues in Alaska [including] law and policy . . . beg to be addressed." In Chapter 2, *Reforming Justice for Alaska Natives: The Time Is Now*,[143] the Commission made several urgent recommendations:

> 2.1: Congress should overturn the U.S. Supreme Court's decision in *Alaska v. Native Village of Venetie Tribal Government* by amending ANCSA to provide that former reservation lands acquired in fee by Alaska Native Villages and other lands transferred in fee to Native villages pursuant to ANCSA are Indian country.

> 2.4: Congress should repeal Section 910 of Title IX of the Violence Against Women Reauthorization Act of 2013 (VAWA Amendments), and thereby permit Alaska Native communities and their courts to address domestic violence and sexual assault committed by tribal members and non-Natives, consistent with the lower forty-eight.

> 2.5: Congress should affirm the inherent criminal jurisdiction of Alaska Native tribal governments over their members within the external boundaries of their villages.

The development and strengthening of local village-based responses is the only assurance that Alaska Native women, and oftentimes their children, living in rural Alaska are provided with the basic human right to safety.

Addressing the Void Created by Concurrent Jurisdiction Between Certain States and American Indian Tribes Created by Congress

> Passage of Public Law 280 did not absolve the federal government of its trust responsibility to Indian nations. The United States has a legal obligation to assist Indian tribes in safeguarding the lives of Native women. This responsibility is not to only some Native women but all Native women.
>
> —Juana Majel Dixon, NCAI First Vice President
> March 2012

A large focus of VAWA 2013 was to expand the Act to reach Native women and other victims so that the lifesaving reforms could reach all communities across the United States. One outstanding area of concern are the issues and severe unmet needs of Native women within an Indian tribe required by federal law, or other acts, to share jurisdiction with a state government. The largest number of Indian tribes sharing concurrent jurisdiction with state governments are those governed by Public Law 83-280 (PL 280), but many other Indian tribes are similarly situated and confront the same realities of inadequate or no access to justice services. In short, state law enforcement, prosecutors, and judicial authorities often do not respond to Native women seeking safety from rapists, batterers, and those committing crimes under VAWA. Further, many Native women seeking health services or other victim services are turned away.

Congress enacted PL 280 in 1953, during the Termination Era. This Act transferred federal criminal justice authority over crimes in Indian country to particular state governments. The Department of Interior, as a policy interpretation, denied access to Indian tribes located within those states to federal funds to develop their respective tribal justice systems. The impact of this policy is that currently when a woman is raped or abused within an Indian tribe located within a PL 280 state no tribal criminal justice agency may be available to assist her. As a result, the perpetrator is free to continue committing horrific violence against the same or different woman. Efforts of the Task Force have included addressing safety for women living within both federal-tribal and state-tribal concurrent jurisdictions. This guiding principle provides a continued recognition of the need to clarify that Indian tribes located within states encompassed under PL 280 or similar legislation have the same authority as other Indian tribes.

During each of the annual USDOJ VAWA consultations (2006–2013), tribal leaders from such tribal-state concurrent jurisdiction presented concerns regarding the lack of state cooperation and failed response to sexual assault, domestic violence, and murder of Native women. Tribal leaders and advocates also raised these issues at numerous USDOJ focus groups, workshops, national conferences, and meetings. The list of concerns regarding the response of state criminal justice agencies to domestic and sexual assault of Native women include the following:

- Slow or no response to emergency calls from tribal communities.
- Refusal to provide law enforcement assistance.
- Refusal to negotiate and amend law enforcement compacts.

- Misinformation on concurrent tribal-state jurisdiction.
- Failure to recognize and enforce tribal orders of protection.
- Failure to prosecute felony domestic and sexual assault crimes.

Addressing the specific barriers to safety for Native women created by Congressional Acts such as PL 280 and Land Claim Settlement Acts, as well as Supreme Court cases, requires national and state reforms. The annual consultation mandate under VAWA 2005 has created a much-needed venue for government-to-government dialogue on these tribal issues of concern. The recommendations listed below are a compilation of those made during the annual VAWA consultations to address the lack of justice services to Native women within PL 280 and similarly situated jurisdictions. They articulate changes needed to advance the safety of Native women, creating systems that adequately deter future violence, and developing tribal justice systems capable of managing such violent crimes.

- Grant Indian tribes' request that the USDOJ reassume felony jurisdiction under the TLOA.
- Develop training on TLOA provisions that permit tribes to request federal resumption of concurrent jurisdiction.
- Assist in developing state-tribal law enforcement compacts that support tribal sovereignty and safety for Indian women, and provide online access to such compacts.
- Provide tribal, federal, and state cross training on implementation of the TLOA specific to tribal-state concurrent jurisdictions.
- In consultation with Indian tribes, develop a protocol for referring federal VAWA crimes to the FBI and U.S. Attorneys located in districts where Indian tribes share concurrent jurisdiction with state governments.
- Provide training for tribal, state, and federal justice personnel on enforcement of VAWA statutes, including the Domestic Assault by an Habitual Offender, Firearms Possession Prohibition, and inter-jurisdictional violations of orders of protection.
- Provide specific training and technical assistance for Indian tribes sharing concurrent jurisdiction with state governments.
- Clarify that VAWA federal offenses occurring within Indian tribes located in PL 280 and similarly situated jurisdictions are investigated and prosecuted by the USDOJ, and train federal and tribal justice personal on federal statutes such as the Domestic Assault by an

Habitual Offender, Firearms Possession Prohibition, and interstate VAWA offenses.

Chapter 5 Notes

[126] National Congress of American Indians, Support for the 2005 Reauthorization of the Violence Against Women Act Including Enhancements for American Indian and Alaska Native Women, Resolution Number PHX-03-034, June 18, 2003.

[127] During the VAWA 2012–2013 reauthorization, NCAI staff attorney Katy Jackson was the Washington, DC, point person for the oftentimes daily issues that needed to be addressed. During the final months before passage, General Counsel John Dosette joined the team to assist in the complicated legal negotiations.

[128] Many elected tribal women leaders actively worked to inform and educate members of Congress about the urgent need for the passage of the tribal amendments during this period including: Councilwoman Terri Henry, Eastern Band of Cherokee Indians; Juana Majel Dixon, Traditional Legislative Counsel Pauma Band of Luiseño Indians; Chairwoman Wanda Batchelor, Washoe Tribe of Nevada and California; Chief Phyllis Anderson, Mississippi Band of Choctaw Indians; Chairwoman LaVonne Peck, La Jolla Band of Luiseno Indians; Vice-Chairwoman Deborah Parker, Tulalip Tribes; and President Fawn Sharp, Quinault Indian Nation.

[129] In addition to the NCAI Task Force the United South and Eastern Tribes are now operating under a resolution of support for initiatives under VAWA.

[130] The Qualla Boundary is territory held in trust by the United States for the Eastern Band of Cherokee Indians in West North Carolina.

[131] In February 2011, the United Nations Special Rapporteur on Women, Rashida Manjoo, accepted the invitation of the NCAI Task Force and the Eastern Band of Cherokee Indians to meet on tribal land and tour tribal programs during her visit to the United States. It was the first visit of a Special Rapporteur on Women to an Indian tribe. Ms. Manjoo included issues and concerns of violence against Indian women within her official report.

[132] NCAI Task Force Co-Chairs Juana Majel and Terri Henry, Tillie Black Bear, Jacqueline Agtuca, and Kiersten Stewart provided the briefing. Special Rapporteur Rashida Manjoo included these findings in her report to the UN High Commission.

[133] Thank-you letter from Tania emailed to the WomenSpirit Coalition of Washington State on May 1, 2013.

[134] S. 1474, Alaska Safe Families and Villages Act of 2013, §2(a)(3).

[135] S. 1474, Alaska Safe Families and Villages Act of 2013, §2(a)(3), (4).

[136] Tami Truett Jerue, *Restoration* Magazine, p. 10 (June 2014). Available at http://restoration.niwrc.org/files/Restoration-V11.2.pdf.

[137] National Platform Discussions Highlight Violence Confronting Alaska Native Women, Restoration Magazine, p. 16 (June 2014). Available at http://restoration.niwrc.org/files/Restoration-V11.2.pdf.

[138] See UAA Justice Center Report to the Council on Domestic Violence and Sexual Assault (May 13, 2010).

[139] See Intimate Partner Violence Against Ahtna Women (August 2006).

[140] See Intimate Partner Violence Against Athabascan Women Residing in Interior Alaska (Nov. 6, 2006).

[141] 522 U.S. 520 (1998).

[142] Nettie Warbelow, *Restoration* Magazine, p. 7 (June 2014). Available at http://restoration.niwrc.org/files/Restoration-V11.2.pdf.

[143] A Roadmap for Making Native American Safer, A Report to the President and Congress of the United States, Chapter 2, Reforming Justice for Alaska Natives, p. 51 (November 2013). Available at http://www.aisc.ucla.edu/iloc/report/files/Chapter_2_Alaska.pdf.

Timeline

Growth of a Movement for the Safety of Native Women 1977–2013

This timeline depicts the milestones in the United States and international community that reflect a growing commitment to increasing the safety of Native women.

1977

- The White Buffalo Calf Woman Society, a tribal women's advocacy organization on the Rosebud Sioux Indian reservation, establishes the first Native women's shelter on an American Indian reservation.[144]

1978

- The U.S. Commission on Civil Rights commissions *Battered Women: Issues of Public Policy*, a document created by activists that compiles 700 pages of written and oral testimony. The document examines the need for a federal role in approaching domestic violence.[145] Tillie Black Bear testifies during the hearings on wife beating regarding domestic violence committed against Native women.
- The National Coalition Against Domestic Violence is founded to provide advocacy and resources for victims of domestic violence.[146] Tillie Black Bear, Sicangu Lakota serves as a founding mother and board member.

1979

- The first Alaska Native Village–based shelter, the Emmonak Women's Shelter, is founded in Yukon Delta Region of Alaska.

1984

- The Family Violence Prevention and Services Act (FVPSA) is authorized, providing federal funding for the first time to help victims of domestic violence and their dependent children by providing support for shelters and related assistance.

1987

- The National Coalition Against Domestic Violence designates October as Domestic Violence Awareness Month.[147]

1990

- Senator Joe Biden introduces the first version of the VAWA to the Senate.

1991

- American Indians Against Abuse is incorporated as the first tribal coalition representing all 11 tribes of Wisconsin.

1994

- The Inter-American Convention on the Prevention, Punishment, and Eradication of Violence Against Women was adopted during a Special Session of the General Assembly of the Organization of American States (OAS). To date, it has been ratified by 34 countries in the Americas.[148]
- VAWA is reintroduced in Congress and enacted with bipartisan support and signed into law on September 13th by President Bill Clinton.

1995

- The Department of Justice creates the Violence Against Women Grants Office to implement VAWA grant programs and the Violence Against Women Policy Office.[149]
- The United Nations 4th World Conference on Women is held in Beijing, China. The Beijing Declaration included the goal to "prevent and eliminate all forms of violence against women and girls."[150]

2000

- VAWA is reauthorized in a bipartisan manner and signed into law by President Clinton. It creates the first federal funding stream for Tribal Domestic Violence and Sexual Assault Coalitions.

2003

- The National Congress of American Indians establishes a National Task Force on Violence Against Native Women.

2005

- VAWA is reauthorized in a bipartisan manner by Congress and signed into law by President George Bush on January 5, 2006. It includes the first title dedicated to safety for Indian Women.

2007

- A coalition of indigenous organizations and individuals submits a collaborative report to the UN Committee on the Elimination of Racial Discrimination (CERD) on the United States' obligations to indigenous peoples, raising the fact that Native women in the U.S. are victims of rape and sexual violence at much higher rates than any other group of women in this country, that most assailants are non-Indians, and that the current criminal jurisdictional scheme created by U.S. law impedes the ability of Indian nations to protect their citizens.[151] The United States ratified the International Convention for the Elimination of All Forms of Racial Discrimination (CERD Convention) in 1994.
- The UN General Assembly adopts the UN Declaration on the Rights of Indigenous Peoples on September 13, 2007, with four countries opposing the Declaration, including the United States.

2008

- A delegation of Native women leaders and other experts[152] attend the February session of CERD in Geneva to highlight the shocking rates of violence against Native women in the United States, and the United States' failure to provide basic law enforcement services in many Native communities.
- CERD responds by issuing Concluding Observations and Recommendations, expressing concern about the high incidence of violence experienced by American Indian and Alaska Native women

and urging the United States to increase its efforts to prevent and punish violence and abuse against Native women in particular.

- Indian organizations, Native women's organizations, tribes, and others working to end violence against Native women file an amicus brief with the Inter-American Commission on Human Rights in support of the plaintiff in *Jessica Lenahan (Gonzales) v. United States,* the first individual case brought by a victim of domestic violence against the United States for international human rights violations.[153]

2009

- President Obama declares April as Sexual Assault Awareness Month.

2010

- The National Indigenous Women's Resource Center is founded.
- President Obama announces the United States' support for the UN Declaration on the Rights of Indigenous Peoples, which is no longer opposed by any country. The Declaration is a powerful affirmation of indigenous rights, including the rights of Native women, as individuals and members of indigenous communities, to gender equality, security of the person, and access to justice. Article 22 of the Declaration is significant for Native women, calling on countries to pay "particular attention" to their special needs and rights in implementing the Declaration and to "take measures, in conjunction with indigenous peoples, to ensure that indigenous women and children enjoy the full protection and guarantees against all forms of violence and discrimination."

2011

- A UN Special Rapporteur on Violence Against Women, Its Causes and Consequences, visits the Eastern Band of Cherokee Indians to examine violence against American Indian women, marking the first visit on tribal lands in the United States,[154] and presents her final report to the UN General Assembly recommending how the United States should prevent and remedy the epidemic of violence against Native women, including restoring tribal authority over all perpetrators who commit acts of sexual or domestic violence on tribal lands.
- At the request of Native women and Indian organizations,[155] the Inter-American Commission on Human Rights holds a first-ever thematic hearing in Washington, DC, on violence against Native women in the

United States. The Commission issued an annex to press release noting its receipt of troubling information about violence against indigenous women and urging countries to diligently address all forms of violence against women.

- The Inter-American Commission on Human Rights issues a landmark decision in *Jessica Lenahan (Gonzales) v. United States*, the first women's human rights case involving domestic violence brought against the United States. The Commission found the United States violated its obligations under international human rights laws by failing to protect Ms. Lenahan and her daughters from violence by her estranged husband. The Commission's decision acknowledges that domestic violence has a disproportionate impact on Native women and takes notice of the amicus brief filed by Indian and Native women's organizations on behalf of many nonprofit organizations and tribal governments.[156]
- The NCAI Task Force on Violence Against Native Women, Sacred Circle National Resource Center to End Violence Against Native Women, and the Indian Law Resource Center submit comments to the State Department on violence against Native women to inform the United States' next report to CERD on its compliance.
- The Senate Committee on Indian Affairs holds a hearing on "Setting the Standard: Domestic Policy Implications of the UN Declaration on the Rights of Indigenous Peoples."
- Senate Committee Indian Affairs Chairman Daniel K. Akaka (D-HI) introduces S. 1763, the Stand Against Violence and Empower Native Women (SAVE Native Women) Act.

2012

- The UN Permanent Forum on Indigenous Issues holds an International Expert Group Meeting in New York City on violence against indigenous women and girls addressing mandates under Article 22 of the UN Declaration on the Rights of Indigenous Peoples. As an invited international indigenous expert, Terri Henry, Tribal Councilwoman for Eastern Band of Cherokee Indians and Co-Chair of the NCAI Task Force on Violence Against Native Women, discusses the epidemic of violence against Native women in the U.S. and how the United States is failing to meet its human rights obligations under the Declaration.

- VAWA 2011 is debated in Congress. Different versions of VAWA pass in the Senate and in the House of Representatives. Congress fails to reauthorize VAWA and the Act remained expired for over 500 days due in part to opposition of some House Republicans to restoring limited criminal jurisdiction to Indian tribes over non-Indians committing domestic violence, dating violence, and violating an order of protection on tribal lands.
- A Special Rapporteur on the Rights of Indigenous Peoples conducts the first mission to United States and issues a report to the UN Human Rights Council acknowledging the alarmingly high rates of violence against Native women in this country and recommending that the U.S. Congress place an immediate priority on legislation, such as VAWA.
- The UN General Assembly adopts a resolution calling for organization of a high-level plenary meeting to be known as the World Conference on Indigenous Peoples, held on September 22–23, 2014, in New York.

2013

- Two international human rights experts call on the United States to reauthorize the Violence Against Women Act, following the Senate's passing of a strengthened bipartisan bill.[157] Rashida Manjoo, Special Rapporteur on Violence Against Women, Its Causes, and Consequences, and James Anaya, Special Rapporteur on the Rights of Indigenous Peoples, emphasize the need for tribal provisions that would enhance protections for Native American and Alaska Native women.
- The UN Permanent Forum on Indigenous Issues releases documents for its 12th Session, including an advance unedited version of a study "on the extent of violence against indigenous women and girls in terms of Article 22(2) of the UN Declaration on the Rights of Indigenous Peoples." [158] The study adopts recommendations issued by the Permanent Forum's international expert group meeting, held in 2012, on violence against indigenous women and girls.
- President Obama signs into law the Violence Against Women Reauthorization Act of 2013, on March 7, 2013, restoring limited criminal jurisdiction of Indian tribes over non-Indians in cases of domestic violence and other important tribal amendments.

Timeline Notes

[144] About Us. (n.d.). *White Buffalo Calf Woman Society, Inc.* Retrieved September 4, 2012, from http://www.wbcws.org/index_files/Page371.htm

[145] U.S. Commission on Civil Rights. (1978). *Battered Women: Issues of Public Policy.* Washington, DC: Government Printing Office.

[146] About NCADV. (n.d.). *National Coalition Against Domestic Violence.* Retrieved September 4, 2012, from http://www.ncadv.org/aboutus.php

[147] Domestic Violence Awareness Month. (n.d.). *National Coalition Against Domestic Violence.* Accessed on September 4, 2012, from http://www.ncadv.org/takeaction/DomesticViolenceAwarenessMonth.php

[148] Inter-American Convention on the Prevention, Punishment and Eradication of Violence Against Women. (1994). *Organization of American States.* Retrieved from http://www.oas.org/juridico/english/treaties/a-61.html

[149] The History of the Violence Against Women Act. (2009). *Office on Violence Against Women.* Retrieved from http://www.ovw.usdoj.gov/docs/history-vawa.pdf

[150] United Nations Fourth World Conference on Women. (1995). *United Nations.* Retrieved from http://www.un.org/womenwatch/daws/beijing/platform/index.html

[151] Report of the Working Group on Indigenous Peoples, submitted to CERD in December 2007 as part of a national report by non-governmental organizations.

[152] The delegation included Vikki Shirley, Navajo Nation First Lady and Navajo Nation Domestic Violence Task Force, Juana Majel Dixon, Pauma Band of Mission Indians and Co-Chair of the NCAI Task Force on Violence Against Native Women, Terri Henry, Director of Clan Star, Inc., and a member of the NCAI Task Force on Violence Against Native Women, and Virginia Davis, Associate Counsel for the NCAI.

[153] The Indian Law Resource Center and Sacred Circle National Resource Center to End Violence Against Native Women filed the amicus brief with the Inter-American Commission on Human Rights in support of the plaintiff in *Jessica Lenahan (Gonzales) v. United States* on behalf of numerous nonprofit organizations and tribal governments working to end violence against Native women.

[154] The visit was co-hosted by NCAI, Clan Star, Inc., Indian Law Resource Center, and Sacred Circle National Resource Center to End Violence Against Native Women.

[155] The request for the hearing was filed by the Indian Law Resource Center, on behalf of itself, the NCAI Task Force on Violence Against Native Women, Clan Star, Inc., and the National Indigenous Women's Resource Center.

[156] The Indian Law Resource Center and Sacred Circle National Resource Center to End Violence Against Native Women filed the amicus brief with the Inter-American Commission on Human Rights in support of the plaintiff in *Jessica*

Lenahan (Gonzales) v. United States, on behalf of numerous nonprofit organizations and tribal governments working to end violence against Native women.

[157] *USA: UN rights experts call on Congress to reauthorize the Violence Against Women Act*, United Nations Human Rights, Office of the High Commissioner for Human Rights, Feb. 19, 2013, http://www.ohchr.org/EN/NewsEvents/Pages/DisplayNews.aspx?NewsID=130 12&LangID=E.

[158] *Study on the extent of violence against indigenous women and girls in terms of article 22(2) of the UN Declaration on the Rights of Indigenous Peoples* is available at http://www.un.org/esa/socdev/unpfii/documents/2013/E_C19_2013_9.pdf

Appendix

VAWA 2013
VAWA 2005, and
Technical Corrections

PUBLIC LAW 113–4—MAR. 7, 2013

VIOLENCE AGAINST WOMEN
REAUTHORIZATION ACT OF 2013
Pages 118 – 126

TITLE IX—SAFETY FOR INDIAN WOMEN

national security officials to be used solely for a national security purpose in a manner that protects the confidentiality of such information.".

(b) GUIDELINES.—Section 384(d) of the Illegal Immigration Reform and Immigrant Responsibility Act of 1996 (8 U.S.C. 1367(d)) is amended—

(1) by inserting ", Secretary of State," after "The Attorney General";

(2) by inserting ", Department of State," after "Department of Justice"; and

(3) by inserting "and severe forms of trafficking in persons or criminal activity listed in section 101(a)(15)(U) of the Immigration and Nationality Act (8 U.S.C. 1101(a)(15)(u))" after "domestic violence".

Deadline.
Guidance.
8 USC 1367 note.

(c) IMPLEMENTATION.—Not later than 180 days after the date of the enactment of this Act, the Attorney General, the Secretary of State, and Secretary of Homeland Security shall provide the guidance required by section 384(d) of the Illegal Immigration Reform and Immigrant Responsibility Act of 1996 (8 U.S.C. 1367(d)), consistent with the amendments made by subsections (a) and (b).

8 USC 1367.

(d) CLERICAL AMENDMENT.—Section 384(a)(1) of the Illegal Immigration Reform and Immigrant Responsibility Act of 1986 is amended by striking "241(a)(2)" in the matter following subparagraph (F) and inserting "237(a)(2)".

TITLE IX—SAFETY FOR INDIAN WOMEN

SEC. 901. GRANTS TO INDIAN TRIBAL GOVERNMENTS.

Section 2015(a) of title I of the Omnibus Crime Control and Safe Streets Act of 1968 (42 U.S.C. 3796gg–10(a)) is amended—

(1) in paragraph (2), by inserting "sex trafficking," after "sexual assault,";

(2) in paragraph (4), by inserting "sex trafficking," after "sexual assault,";

(3) in paragraph (5), by striking "and stalking" and all that follows and inserting "sexual assault, sex trafficking, and stalking;";

(4) in paragraph (7)—

(A) by inserting "sex trafficking," after "sexual assault," each place it appears; and

(B) by striking "and" at the end;

(5) in paragraph (8)—

(A) by inserting "sex trafficking," after "stalking,"; and

(B) by striking the period at the end and inserting a semicolon; and

(6) by adding at the end the following:

"(9) provide services to address the needs of youth who are victims of domestic violence, dating violence, sexual assault, sex trafficking, or stalking and the needs of youth and children exposed to domestic violence, dating violence, sexual assault, or stalking, including support for the nonabusing parent or the caretaker of the youth or child; and

"(10) develop and promote legislation and policies that enhance best practices for responding to violent crimes against Indian women, including the crimes of domestic violence, dating violence, sexual assault, sex trafficking, and stalking.".

PUBLIC LAW 113–4—MAR. 7, 2013   127 STAT. 119

SEC. 902. GRANTS TO INDIAN TRIBAL COALITIONS.

Section 2001 of title I of the Omnibus Crime Control and Safe Streets Act of 1968 (42 U.S.C. 3796gg) is amended by striking subsection (d) and inserting the following:

"(d) TRIBAL COALITION GRANTS.—

"(1) PURPOSE.—The Attorney General shall award a grant to tribal coalitions for purposes of—

"(A) increasing awareness of domestic violence and sexual assault against Indian women;

"(B) enhancing the response to violence against Indian women at the Federal, State, and tribal levels;

"(C) identifying and providing technical assistance to coalition membership and tribal communities to enhance access to essential services to Indian women victimized by domestic and sexual violence, including sex trafficking; and

"(D) assisting Indian tribes in developing and promoting State, local, and tribal legislation and policies that enhance best practices for responding to violent crimes against Indian women, including the crimes of domestic violence, dating violence, sexual assault, sex trafficking, and stalking.

"(2) GRANTS.—The Attorney General shall award grants on an annual basis under paragraph (1) to—

"(A) each tribal coalition that—

"(i) meets the criteria of a tribal coalition under section 40002(a) of the Violence Against Women Act of 1994 (42 U.S.C. 13925(a));

"(ii) is recognized by the Office on Violence Against Women; and

"(iii) provides services to Indian tribes; and

"(B) organizations that propose to incorporate and operate a tribal coalition in areas where Indian tribes are located but no tribal coalition exists.

"(3) USE OF AMOUNTS.—For each of fiscal years 2014 through 2018, of the amounts appropriated to carry out this subsection—

"(A) not more than 10 percent shall be made available to organizations described in paragraph (2)(B), provided that 1 or more organizations determined by the Attorney General to be qualified apply;

"(B) not less than 90 percent shall be made available to tribal coalitions described in paragraph (2)(A), which amounts shall be distributed equally among each eligible tribal coalition for the applicable fiscal year.

"(4) ELIGIBILITY FOR OTHER GRANTS.—Receipt of an award under this subsection by a tribal coalition shall not preclude the tribal coalition from receiving additional grants under this title to carry out the purposes described in paragraph (1).

"(5) MULTIPLE PURPOSE APPLICATIONS.—Nothing in this subsection prohibits any tribal coalition or organization described in paragraph (2) from applying for funding to address sexual assault or domestic violence needs in the same application.".

Applicability.

150

SEC. 903. CONSULTATION.

Section 903 of the Violence Against Women and Department of Justice Reauthorization Act of 2005 (42 U.S.C. 14045d) is amended—

(1) in subsection (a)—

(A) by striking "and the Violence Against Women Act of 2000" and inserting ", the Violence Against Women Act of 2000"; and

(B) by inserting ", and the Violence Against Women Reauthorization Act of 2013" before the period at the end;

(2) in subsection (b)—

(A) in the matter preceding paragraph (1), by striking "Secretary of the Department of Health and Human Services" and inserting "Secretary of Health and Human Services, the Secretary of the Interior,"; and

(B) in paragraph (2), by striking "and stalking" and inserting "stalking, and sex trafficking"; and

(3) by adding at the end the following:

"(c) ANNUAL REPORT.—The Attorney General shall submit to Congress an annual report on the annual consultations required under subsection (a) that—

"(1) contains the recommendations made under subsection (b) by Indian tribes during the year covered by the report;

"(2) describes actions taken during the year covered by the report to respond to recommendations made under subsection (b) during the year or a previous year; and

"(3) describes how the Attorney General will work in coordination and collaboration with Indian tribes, the Secretary of Health and Human Services, and the Secretary of the Interior to address the recommendations made under subsection (b).

Deadline.

"(d) NOTICE.—Not later than 120 days before the date of a consultation under subsection (a), the Attorney General shall notify tribal leaders of the date, time, and location of the consultation.".

SEC. 904. TRIBAL JURISDICTION OVER CRIMES OF DOMESTIC VIOLENCE.

Title II of Public Law 90–284 (25 U.S.C. 1301 et seq.) (commonly known as the "Indian Civil Rights Act of 1968") is amended by adding at the end the following:

25 USC 1304.

"SEC. 204. TRIBAL JURISDICTION OVER CRIMES OF DOMESTIC VIOLENCE.

"(a) DEFINITIONS.—In this section:

"(1) DATING VIOLENCE.—The term 'dating violence' means violence committed by a person who is or has been in a social relationship of a romantic or intimate nature with the victim, as determined by the length of the relationship, the type of relationship, and the frequency of interaction between the persons involved in the relationship.

"(2) DOMESTIC VIOLENCE.—The term 'domestic violence' means violence committed by a current or former spouse or intimate partner of the victim, by a person with whom the victim shares a child in common, by a person who is cohabitating with or has cohabitated with the victim as a spouse or intimate partner, or by a person similarly situated to a spouse of the victim under the domestic- or family- violence laws of an Indian tribe that has jurisdiction over the Indian country where the violence occurs.

"(3) INDIAN COUNTRY.—The term 'Indian country' has the meaning given the term in section 1151 of title 18, United States Code.

"(4) PARTICIPATING TRIBE.—The term 'participating tribe' means an Indian tribe that elects to exercise special domestic violence criminal jurisdiction over the Indian country of that Indian tribe.

"(5) PROTECTION ORDER.—The term 'protection order'—

"(A) means any injunction, restraining order, or other order issued by a civil or criminal court for the purpose of preventing violent or threatening acts or harassment against, sexual violence against, contact or communication with, or physical proximity to, another person; and

"(B) includes any temporary or final order issued by a civil or criminal court, whether obtained by filing an independent action or as a pendent lite order in another proceeding, if the civil or criminal order was issued in response to a complaint, petition, or motion filed by or on behalf of a person seeking protection.

"(6) SPECIAL DOMESTIC VIOLENCE CRIMINAL JURISDICTION.— The term 'special domestic violence criminal jurisdiction' means the criminal jurisdiction that a participating tribe may exercise under this section but could not otherwise exercise.

"(7) SPOUSE OR INTIMATE PARTNER.—The term 'spouse or intimate partner' has the meaning given the term in section 2266 of title 18, United States Code.

"(b) NATURE OF THE CRIMINAL JURISDICTION.—

"(1) IN GENERAL.—Notwithstanding any other provision of law, in addition to all powers of self-government recognized and affirmed by sections 201 and 203, the powers of self-government of a participating tribe include the inherent power of that tribe, which is hereby recognized and affirmed, to exercise special domestic violence criminal jurisdiction over all persons.

"(2) CONCURRENT JURISDICTION.—The exercise of special domestic violence criminal jurisdiction by a participating tribe shall be concurrent with the jurisdiction of the United States, of a State, or of both.

"(3) APPLICABILITY.—Nothing in this section—

"(A) creates or eliminates any Federal or State criminal jurisdiction over Indian country; or

"(B) affects the authority of the United States or any State government that has been delegated authority by the United States to investigate and prosecute a criminal violation in Indian country.

"(4) EXCEPTIONS.—

"(A) VICTIM AND DEFENDANT ARE BOTH NON-INDIANS.—

"(i) IN GENERAL.—A participating tribe may not exercise special domestic violence criminal jurisdiction over an alleged offense if neither the defendant nor the alleged victim is an Indian.

"(ii) DEFINITION OF VICTIM.—In this subparagraph and with respect to a criminal proceeding in which a participating tribe exercises special domestic violence criminal jurisdiction based on a violation of a protection order, the term 'victim' means a person specifically protected by a protection order that the defendant allegedly violated.

"(B) DEFENDANT LACKS TIES TO THE INDIAN TRIBE.— A participating tribe may exercise special domestic violence criminal jurisdiction over a defendant only if the defendant—

"(i) resides in the Indian country of the participating tribe;

"(ii) is employed in the Indian country of the participating tribe; or

"(iii) is a spouse, intimate partner, or dating partner of—

"(I) a member of the participating tribe; or

"(II) an Indian who resides in the Indian country of the participating tribe.

"(c) CRIMINAL CONDUCT.—A participating tribe may exercise special domestic violence criminal jurisdiction over a defendant for criminal conduct that falls into one or more of the following categories:

"(1) DOMESTIC VIOLENCE AND DATING VIOLENCE.—An act of domestic violence or dating violence that occurs in the Indian country of the participating tribe.

"(2) VIOLATIONS OF PROTECTION ORDERS.—An act that—

"(A) occurs in the Indian country of the participating tribe; and

"(B) violates the portion of a protection order that—

"(i) prohibits or provides protection against violent or threatening acts or harassment against, sexual violence against, contact or communication with, or physical proximity to, another person;

"(ii) was issued against the defendant;

"(iii) is enforceable by the participating tribe; and

"(iv) is consistent with section 2265(b) of title 18, United States Code.

"(d) RIGHTS OF DEFENDANTS.—In a criminal proceeding in which a participating tribe exercises special domestic violence criminal jurisdiction, the participating tribe shall provide to the defendant—

"(1) all applicable rights under this Act;

"(2) if a term of imprisonment of any length may be imposed, all rights described in section 202(c);

"(3) the right to a trial by an impartial jury that is drawn from sources that—

"(A) reflect a fair cross section of the community; and

"(B) do not systematically exclude any distinctive group in the community, including non-Indians; and

"(4) all other rights whose protection is necessary under the Constitution of the United States in order for Congress to recognize and affirm the inherent power of the participating tribe to exercise special domestic violence criminal jurisdiction over the defendant.

"(e) PETITIONS TO STAY DETENTION.—

"(1) IN GENERAL.—A person who has filed a petition for a writ of habeas corpus in a court of the United States under section 203 may petition that court to stay further detention of that person by the participating tribe.

"(2) GRANT OF STAY.—A court shall grant a stay described in paragraph (1) if the court—

"(A) finds that there is a substantial likelihood that the habeas corpus petition will be granted; and

"(B) after giving each alleged victim in the matter an opportunity to be heard, finds by clear and convincing evidence that under conditions imposed by the court, the petitioner is not likely to flee or pose a danger to any person or the community if released.

"(3) NOTICE.—An Indian tribe that has ordered the detention of any person has a duty to timely notify such person of his rights and privileges under this subsection and under section 203.

"(f) GRANTS TO TRIBAL GOVERNMENTS.—The Attorney General may award grants to the governments of Indian tribes (or to authorized designees of those governments)—

"(1) to strengthen tribal criminal justice systems to assist Indian tribes in exercising special domestic violence criminal jurisdiction, including—

"(A) law enforcement (including the capacity of law enforcement or court personnel to enter information into and obtain information from national crime information databases);

"(B) prosecution;

"(C) trial and appellate courts;

"(D) probation systems;

"(E) detention and correctional facilities;

"(F) alternative rehabilitation centers;

"(G) culturally appropriate services and assistance for victims and their families; and

"(H) criminal codes and rules of criminal procedure, appellate procedure, and evidence;

"(2) to provide indigent criminal defendants with the effective assistance of licensed defense counsel, at no cost to the defendant, in criminal proceedings in which a participating tribe prosecutes a crime of domestic violence or dating violence or a criminal violation of a protection order;

"(3) to ensure that, in criminal proceedings in which a participating tribe exercises special domestic violence criminal jurisdiction, jurors are summoned, selected, and instructed in a manner consistent with all applicable requirements; and

"(4) to accord victims of domestic violence, dating violence, and violations of protection orders rights that are similar to the rights of a crime victim described in section 3771(a) of title 18, United States Code, consistent with tribal law and custom.

"(g) SUPPLEMENT, NOT SUPPLANT.—Amounts made available under this section shall supplement and not supplant any other Federal, State, tribal, or local government amounts made available to carry out activities described in this section.

"(h) AUTHORIZATION OF APPROPRIATIONS.—There are authorized to be appropriated $5,000,000 for each of fiscal years 2014 through 2018 to carry out subsection (f) and to provide training, technical assistance, data collection, and evaluation of the criminal justice systems of participating tribes.".

SEC. 905. TRIBAL PROTECTION ORDERS.

Section 2265 of title 18, United States Code, is amended by striking subsection (e) and inserting the following:

"(e) TRIBAL COURT JURISDICTION.—For purposes of this section, a court of an Indian tribe shall have full civil jurisdiction to issue and enforce protection orders involving any person, including the authority to enforce any orders through civil contempt proceedings, to exclude violators from Indian land, and to use other appropriate mechanisms, in matters arising anywhere in the Indian country of the Indian tribe (as defined in section 1151) or otherwise within the authority of the Indian tribe.".

SEC. 906. AMENDMENTS TO THE FEDERAL ASSAULT STATUTE.

(a) IN GENERAL.—Section 113 of title 18, United States Code, is amended—

(1) in subsection (a)—

(A) by striking paragraph (1) and inserting the following:

"(1) Assault with intent to commit murder or a violation of section 2241 or 2242, by a fine under this title, imprisonment for not more than 20 years, or both.";

(B) in paragraph (2), by striking "felony under chapter 109A" and inserting "violation of section 2241 or 2242";

(C) in paragraph (3) by striking "and without just cause or excuse,";

(D) in paragraph (4), by striking "six months" and inserting "1 year";

(E) in paragraph (7)—

(i) by striking "substantial bodily injury to an individual who has not attained the age of 16 years" and inserting "substantial bodily injury to a spouse or intimate partner, a dating partner, or an individual who has not attained the age of 16 years"; and

(ii) by striking "fine" and inserting "a fine"; and

(F) by adding at the end the following:

"(8) Assault of a spouse, intimate partner, or dating partner by strangling, suffocating, or attempting to strangle or suffocate, by a fine under this title, imprisonment for not more than 10 years, or both."; and

(2) in subsection (b)—

(A) by striking "(b) As used in this subsection—" and inserting the following:

"(b) DEFINITIONS.—In this section—";

(B) in paragraph (1)(B), by striking "and" at the end;

(C) in paragraph (2), by striking the period at the end and inserting a semicolon; and

(D) by adding at the end the following:

"(3) the terms 'dating partner' and 'spouse or intimate partner' have the meanings given those terms in section 2266;

"(4) the term 'strangling' means intentionally, knowingly, or recklessly impeding the normal breathing or circulation of the blood of a person by applying pressure to the throat or neck, regardless of whether that conduct results in any visible injury or whether there is any intent to kill or protractedly injure the victim; and

"(5) the term 'suffocating' means intentionally, knowingly, or recklessly impeding the normal breathing of a person by covering the mouth of the person, the nose of the person, or both, regardless of whether that conduct results in any visible injury or whether there is any intent to kill or protractedly injure the victim.".

(b) INDIAN MAJOR CRIMES.—Section 1153(a) of title 18, United States Code, is amended by striking "assault with intent to commit murder, assault with a dangerous weapon, assault resulting in serious bodily injury (as defined in section 1365 of this title)" and inserting "a felony assault under section 113".

(c) REPEAT OFFENDERS.—Section 2265A(b)(1)(B) of title 18, United States Code, is amended by inserting "or tribal" after "State".

SEC. 907. ANALYSIS AND RESEARCH ON VIOLENCE AGAINST INDIAN WOMEN.

(a) IN GENERAL.—Section 904(a) of the Violence Against Women and Department of Justice Reauthorization Act of 2005 (42 U.S.C. 3796gg–10 note) is amended—

(1) in paragraph (1)—
(A) by striking "The National" and inserting "Not later than 2 years after the date of enactment of the Violence Against Women Reauthorization Act of 2013, the National"; and
(B) by inserting "and in Native villages (as defined in section 3 of the Alaska Native Claims Settlement Act (43 U.S.C. 1602))" before the period at the end;
(2) in paragraph (2)(A)—
(A) in clause (iv), by striking "and" at the end;
(B) in clause (v), by striking the period at the end and inserting "; and"; and
(C) by adding at the end the following:
"(vi) sex trafficking.";
(3) in paragraph (4), by striking "this Act" and inserting "the Violence Against Women Reauthorization Act of 2013"; and
(4) in paragraph (5), by striking "this section $1,000,000 for each of fiscal years 2007 and 2008" and inserting "this subsection $1,000,000 for each of fiscal years 2014 and 2015".

(b) AUTHORIZATION OF APPROPRIATIONS.—Section 905(b)(2) of the Violence Against Women and Department of Justice Reauthorization Act of 2005 (28 U.S.C. 534 note) is amended by striking "fiscal years 2007 through 2011" and inserting "fiscal years 2014 through 2018".

SEC. 908. EFFECTIVE DATES; PILOT PROJECT.

25 USC 1304 note.

(a) GENERAL EFFECTIVE DATE.—Except as provided in section 4 and subsection (b) of this section, the amendments made by this title shall take effect on the date of enactment of this Act.

(b) EFFECTIVE DATE FOR SPECIAL DOMESTIC-VIOLENCE CRIMINAL JURISDICTION.—

(1) IN GENERAL.—Except as provided in paragraph (2), subsections (b) through (d) of section 204 of Public Law 90–284 (as added by section 904) shall take effect on the date that is 2 years after the date of enactment of this Act.

(2) PILOT PROJECT.—

(A) IN GENERAL.—At any time during the 2-year period beginning on the date of enactment of this Act, an Indian tribe may ask the Attorney General to designate the tribe

Time period.

as a participating tribe under section 204(a) of Public Law 90–284 on an accelerated basis.

(B) PROCEDURE.—The Attorney General may grant a request under subparagraph (A) after coordinating with the Secretary of the Interior, consulting with affected Indian tribes, and concluding that the criminal justice system of the requesting tribe has adequate safeguards in place to protect defendants' rights, consistent with section 204 of Public Law 90–284.

Consultation.
Deadline.

(C) EFFECTIVE DATES FOR PILOT PROJECTS.—An Indian tribe designated as a participating tribe under this paragraph may commence exercising special domestic violence criminal jurisdiction pursuant to subsections (b) through (d) of section 204 of Public Law 90–284 on a date established by the Attorney General, after consultation with that Indian tribe, but in no event later than the date that is 2 years after the date of enactment of this Act.

SEC. 909. INDIAN LAW AND ORDER COMMISSION; REPORT ON THE ALASKA RURAL JUSTICE AND LAW ENFORCEMENT COMMISSION.

(a) IN GENERAL.—Section 15(f) of the Indian Law Enforcement Reform Act (25 U.S.C. 2812(f)) is amended by striking "2 years" and inserting "3 years".

Consultation.

(b) REPORT.—The Attorney General, in consultation with the Attorney General of the State of Alaska, the Commissioner of Public Safety of the State of Alaska, the Alaska Federation of Natives and Federally recognized Indian tribes in the State of Alaska, shall report to Congress not later than one year after enactment of this Act with respect to whether the Alaska Rural Justice and Law Enforcement Commission established under Section 112(a)(1) of the Consolidated Appropriations Act, 2004 should be continued and appropriations authorized for the continued work of the commission. The report may contain recommendations for legislation with respect to the scope of work and composition of the commission.

18 USC 2265 note.
Applicability.

SEC. 910. SPECIAL RULE FOR THE STATE OF ALASKA.

(a) EXPANDED JURISDICTION.—In the State of Alaska, the amendments made by sections 904 and 905 shall only apply to the Indian country (as defined in section 1151 of title 18, United States Code) of the Metlakatla Indian Community, Annette Island Reserve.

(b) RETAINED JURISDICTION.—The jurisdiction and authority of each Indian tribe in the State of Alaska under section 2265(e) of title 18, United States Code (as in effect on the day before the date of enactment of this Act)—

(1) shall remain in full force and effect; and

(2) are not limited or diminished by this Act or any amendment made by this Act.

(c) SAVINGS PROVISION.—Nothing in this Act or an amendment made by this Act limits or diminishes the jurisdiction of the State of Alaska, any subdivision of the State of Alaska, or any Indian tribe in the State of Alaska.

PUBLIC LAW 109–162—JAN. 5, 2006

VIOLENCE AGAINST WOMEN AND DEPARTMENT OF JUSTICE REAUTHORIZATION ACT OF 2005

Pages 3077 – 3084

TITLE IX—SAFETY FOR INDIAN WOMEN

from clients and petitioners by international marriage brokers, the Department of State, or the Department of Homeland Security;

(D) that examines, based on the information gathered, the extent to which persons with a history of violence are using either the K nonimmigrant visa process or the services of international marriage brokers, or both, and the extent to which such persons are providing accurate and complete information to the Department of State or the Department of Homeland Security and to international marriage brokers in accordance with subsections (a) and (d)(2)(B); and

(E) that assesses the accuracy and completeness of the criminal background check performed by the Secretary of Homeland Security at identifying past instances of domestic violence.

(2) REPORT.—Not later than 2 years after the date of enactment of this Act, the Comptroller General shall submit to the Committee on the Judiciary of the Senate and the Committee on the Judiciary of the House of Representatives a report setting forth the results of the study conducted under paragraph (1).

(3) DATA COLLECTION.—The Secretary of Homeland Security and the Secretary of State shall collect and maintain the data necessary for the Comptroller General of the United States to conduct the study required by paragraph (1).

(g) REPEAL OF MAIL-ORDER BRIDE PROVISION.—Section 652 of the Illegal Immigration Reform and Immigrant Responsibility Act of 1996 (division C of Public Law 104–208; 8 U.S.C. 1375) is hereby repealed.

SEC. 834. SHARING OF CERTAIN INFORMATION.   8 USC 1202 note.

Section 222(f) of the Immigration and Nationality Act (8 U.S.C. 1202(f)) shall not be construed to prevent the sharing of information regarding a United States petitioner for a visa under clause (i) or (ii) of section 101(a)(15)(K) of such Act (8 U.S.C. 1101(a)(15)(K)) for the limited purposes of fulfilling disclosure obligations imposed by the amendments made by section 832(a) or by section 833, including reporting obligations of the Comptroller General of the United States under section 833(f).

TITLE IX—SAFETY FOR INDIAN WOMEN

SEC. 901. FINDINGS.   42 USC
                            3796gg–10 note.
Congress finds that—

(1) 1 out of every 3 Indian (including Alaska Native) women are raped in their lifetimes;

(2) Indian women experience 7 sexual assaults per 1,000, compared with 4 per 1,000 among Black Americans, 3 per 1,000 among Caucasians, 2 per 1,000 among Hispanic women, and 1 per 1,000 among Asian women;

(3) Indian women experience the violent crime of battering at a rate of 23.2 per 1,000, compared with 8 per 1,000 among Caucasian women;

(4) during the period 1979 through 1992, homicide was the third leading cause of death of Indian females aged 15

to 34, and 75 percent were killed by family members or acquaintances;

(5) Indian tribes require additional criminal justice and victim services resources to respond to violent assaults against women; and

(6) the unique legal relationship of the United States to Indian tribes creates a Federal trust responsibility to assist tribal governments in safeguarding the lives of Indian women.

42 USC 3796gg–10 note.

SEC. 902. PURPOSES.

The purposes of this title are—

(1) to decrease the incidence of violent crimes against Indian women;

(2) to strengthen the capacity of Indian tribes to exercise their sovereign authority to respond to violent crimes committed against Indian women; and

(3) to ensure that perpetrators of violent crimes committed against Indian women are held accountable for their criminal behavior.

42 USC 14045d.

SEC. 903. CONSULTATION.

(a) IN GENERAL.—The Attorney General shall conduct annual consultations with Indian tribal governments concerning the Federal administration of tribal funds and programs established under this Act, the Violence Against Women Act of 1994 (title IV of Public Law 103–322; 108 Stat. 1902) and the Violence Against Women Act of 2000 (division B of Public Law 106–386; 114 Stat. 1491).

(b) RECOMMENDATIONS.—During consultations under subsection (a), the Secretary of the Department of Health and Human Services and the Attorney General shall solicit recommendations from Indian tribes concerning—

(1) administering tribal funds and programs;

(2) enhancing the safety of Indian women from domestic violence, dating violence, sexual assault, and stalking; and

(3) strengthening the Federal response to such violent crimes.

SEC. 904. ANALYSIS AND RESEARCH ON VIOLENCE AGAINST INDIAN WOMEN.

42 USC 3796gg–10 note.

(a) NATIONAL BASELINE STUDY —

(1) IN GENERAL.—The National Institute of Justice, in consultation with the Office on Violence Against Women, shall conduct a national baseline study to examine violence against Indian women in Indian country.

(2) SCOPE.—

(A) IN GENERAL.—The study shall examine violence committed against Indian women, including—

(i) domestic violence;
(ii) dating violence;
(iii) sexual assault;
(iv) stalking; and
(v) murder.

(B) EVALUATION.—The study shall evaluate the effectiveness of Federal, State, tribal, and local responses to the violations described in subparagraph (A) committed against Indian women.

(C) RECOMMENDATIONS.—The study shall propose recommendations to improve the effectiveness of Federal, State, tribal, and local responses to the violation described in subparagraph (A) committed against Indian women.

(3) TASK FORCE.—

Establishment.

(A) IN GENERAL.—The Attorney General, acting through the Director of the Office on Violence Against Women, shall establish a task force to assist in the development and implementation of the study under paragraph (1) and guide implementation of the recommendation in paragraph (2)(C).

(B) MEMBERS.—The Director shall appoint to the task force representatives from—

(i) national tribal domestic violence and sexual assault nonprofit organizations;

(ii) tribal governments; and

(iii) the national tribal organizations.

(4) REPORT.—Not later than 2 years after the date of enactment of this Act, the Attorney General shall submit to the Committee on Indian Affairs of the Senate, the Committee on the Judiciary of the Senate, and the Committee on the Judiciary of the House of Representatives a report that describes the study.

(5) AUTHORIZATION OF APPROPRIATIONS.—There is authorized to be appropriated to carry out this section $1,000,000 for each of fiscal years 2007 and 2008, to remain available until expended.

(b) INJURY STUDY.—

(1) IN GENERAL.—The Secretary of Health and Human Services, acting through the Indian Health Service and the Centers for Disease Control and Prevention, shall conduct a study to obtain a national projection of—

(A) the incidence of injuries and homicides resulting from domestic violence, dating violence, sexual assault, or stalking committed against American Indian and Alaska Native women; and

(B) the cost of providing health care for the injuries described in subparagraph (A).

(2) REPORT.—Not later than 2 years after the date of enactment of this Act, the Secretary of Health and Human Services shall submit to the Committee on Indian Affairs of the Senate, the Committee on the Judiciary of the Senate, and the Committee on the Judiciary of the House of Representatives a report that describes the findings made in the study and recommends health care strategies for reducing the incidence and cost of the injuries described in paragraph (1).

(3) AUTHORIZATION OF APPROPRIATIONS.—There is authorized to be appropriated to carry out this section $500,000 for each of fiscal years 2007 and 2008, to remain available until expended.

SEC. 905. TRACKING OF VIOLENCE AGAINST INDIAN WOMEN.

(a) ACCESS TO FEDERAL CRIMINAL INFORMATION DATABASES.—Section 534 of title 28, United States Code, is amended—

(1) by redesignating subsection (d) as subsection (e); and

(2) by inserting after subsection (c) the following:

"(d) INDIAN LAW ENFORCEMENT AGENCIES.—The Attorney General shall permit Indian law enforcement agencies, in cases of domestic violence, dating violence, sexual assault, and stalking, to enter information into Federal criminal information databases and to obtain information from the databases.".

28 USC 534 note.

(b) TRIBAL REGISTRY.—

(1) ESTABLISHMENT.—The Attorney General shall contract with any interested Indian tribe, tribal organization, or tribal nonprofit organization to develop and maintain—

(A) a national tribal sex offender registry; and

(B) a tribal protection order registry containing civil and criminal orders of protection issued by Indian tribes and participating jurisdictions.

(2) AUTHORIZATION OF APPROPRIATIONS.—There is authorized to be appropriated to carry out this section $1,000,000 for each of fiscal years 2007 through 2011, to remain available until expended.

SEC. 906. GRANTS TO INDIAN TRIBAL GOVERNMENTS.

(a) IN GENERAL.—Part T of title I of the Omnibus Crime Control and Safe Streets Act of 1968 (42 U.S.C. 3796gg et seq.) is amended by adding at the end the following:

42 USC
3796gg–10.

"SEC. 2007. GRANTS TO INDIAN TRIBAL GOVERNMENTS.

"(a) GRANTS.—The Attorney General may make grants to Indian tribal governments and tribal organizations to—

"(1) develop and enhance effective governmental strategies to curtail violent crimes against and increase the safety of Indian women consistent with tribal law and custom;

"(2) increase tribal capacity to respond to domestic violence, dating violence, sexual assault, and stalking crimes against Indian women;

"(3) strengthen tribal justice interventions including tribal law enforcement, prosecution, courts, probation, correctional facilities;

"(4) enhance services to Indian women victimized by domestic violence, dating violence, sexual assault, and stalking;

"(5) work in cooperation with the community to develop education and prevention strategies directed toward issues of domestic violence, dating violence, and stalking programs and to address the needs of children exposed to domestic violence;

"(6) provide programs for supervised visitation and safe visitation exchange of children in situations involving domestic violence, sexual assault, or stalking committed by one parent against the other with appropriate security measures, policies, and procedures to protect the safety of victims and their children; and

"(7) provide transitional housing for victims of domestic violence, dating violence, sexual assault, or stalking, including rental or utilities payments assistance and assistance with related expenses such as security deposits and other costs incidental to relocation to transitional housing, and support services to enable a victim of domestic violence, dating violence, sexual assault, or stalking to locate and secure permanent housing and integrate into a community.

"(b) COLLABORATION.—All applicants under this section shall demonstrate their proposal was developed in consultation with a nonprofit, nongovernmental Indian victim services program, including sexual assault and domestic violence victim services providers in the tribal or local community, or a nonprofit tribal domestic violence and sexual assault coalition to the extent that they exist. In the absence of such a demonstration, the applicant may meet the requirement of this subsection through consultation with women in the community to be served.

"(c) NONEXCLUSIVITY.—The Federal share of a grant made under this section may not exceed 90 percent of the total costs of the project described in the application submitted, except that the Attorney General may grant a waiver of this match requirement on the basis of demonstrated financial hardship. Funds appropriated for the activities of any agency of an Indian tribal government or of the Bureau of Indian Affairs performing law enforcement functions on any Indian lands may be used to provide the non-Federal share of the cost of programs or projects funded under this section.".

(b) AUTHORIZATION OF FUNDS FROM GRANTS TO COMBAT VIOLENT CRIMES AGAINST WOMEN.—Section 2007(b)(1) of the Omnibus Crime Control and Safe Streets Act of 1968 (42 U.S.C. 3796gg–1(b)(1)) is amended to read as follows:

"(1) Ten percent shall be available for grants under the program authorized in section 2007. The requirements of this part shall not apply to funds allocated for such program.".

(c) AUTHORIZATION OF FUNDS FROM GRANTS TO ENCOURAGE STATE POLICIES AND ENFORCEMENT OF PROTECTION ORDERS PROGRAM.—Section 2101 of the Omnibus Crime Control and Safe Streets Act of 1968 (42 U.S.C. 3796hh) is amended by striking subsection (e) and inserting the following:

"(e) Not less than 10 percent of the total amount available under this section for each fiscal year shall be available for grants under the program authorized in section 2007. The requirements of this part shall not apply to funds allocated for such program.".

(d) AUTHORIZATION OF FUNDS FROM RURAL DOMESTIC VIOLENCE AND CHILD ABUSE ENFORCEMENT ASSISTANCE GRANTS.—Subsection 40295(c) of the Violence Against Women Act of 1994 (42 U.S.C. 13971(c)(3)) is amended by striking paragraph (3) and inserting the following:

"(3) Not less than 10 percent of the total amount available under this section for each fiscal year shall be available for grants under the program authorized in section 2007 of the Omnibus Crime Control and Safe Streets Act of 1968. The requirements of this paragraph shall not apply to funds allocated for such program.".

(e) AUTHORIZATION OF FUNDS FROM THE SAFE HAVENS FOR CHILDREN PROGRAM.—Section 1301 of the Violence Against Women Act of 2000 (42 U.S.C. 10420) is amended by striking subsection (f) and inserting the following:

"(f) Not less than 10 percent of the total amount available under this section for each fiscal year shall be available for grants under the program authorized in section 2007 of the Omnibus Crime Control and Safe Streets Act of 1968. The requirements of this subsection shall not apply to funds allocated for such program.".

(f) AUTHORIZATION OF FUNDS FROM THE TRANSITIONAL HOUSING ASSISTANCE GRANTS FOR CHILD VICTIMS OF DOMESTIC VIOLENCE, STALKING, OR SEXUAL ASSAULT PROGRAM.—Section 40299(g) of the

Violence Against Women Act of 1994 (42 U.S.C. 13975(g)) is amended by adding at the end the following:

"(4) TRIBAL PROGRAM.—Not less than 10 percent of the total amount available under this section for each fiscal year shall be available for grants under the program authorized in section 2007 of the Omnibus Crime Control and Safe Streets Act of 1968. The requirements of this paragraph shall not apply to funds allocated for such program.".

(g) AUTHORIZATION OF FUNDS FROM THE LEGAL ASSISTANCE FOR VICTIMS IMPROVEMENTS PROGRAM.—Section 1201(f) of the Violence Against Women Act of 2000 (42 U.S.C. 3796gg–6) is amended by adding at the end the following:

"(4) Not less than 10 percent of the total amount available under this section for each fiscal year shall be available for grants under the program authorized in section 2007 of the Omnibus Crime Control and Safe Streets Act of 1968. The requirements of this paragraph shall not apply to funds allocated for such program.".

SEC. 907. TRIBAL DEPUTY IN THE OFFICE ON VIOLENCE AGAINST WOMEN.

Part T of title I of the Omnibus Crime Control and Safe Streets Act of 1968 (42 U.S.C. 3796gg et seq.), as amended by section 906, is amended by adding at the end the following:

42 USC 3796gg–11.

"SEC. 2008. TRIBAL DEPUTY.

"(a) ESTABLISHMENT.—There is established in the Office on Violence Against Women a Deputy Director for Tribal Affairs.

"(b) DUTIES.—

"(1) IN GENERAL.—The Deputy Director shall under the guidance and authority of the Director of the Office on Violence Against Women—

Grants.
Contracts.

"(A) oversee and manage the administration of grants to and contracts with Indian tribes, tribal courts, tribal organizations, or tribal nonprofit organizations;

"(B) ensure that, if a grant under this Act or a contract pursuant to such a grant is made to an organization to perform services that benefit more than 1 Indian tribe, the approval of each Indian tribe to be benofitted shall be a prerequisite to the making of the grant or letting of the contract;

Guidelines.

"(C) coordinate development of Federal policy, protocols, and guidelines on matters relating to violence against Indian women;

"(D) advise the Director of the Office on Violence Against Women concerning policies, legislation, implementation of laws, and other issues relating to violence against Indian women;

"(E) represent the Office on Violence Against Women in the annual consultations under section 903;

"(F) provide technical assistance, coordination, and support to other offices and bureaus in the Department of Justice to develop policy and to enforce Federal laws relating to violence against Indian women, including through litigation of civil and criminal actions relating to those laws;

"(G) maintain a liaison with the judicial branches of Federal, State, and tribal governments on matters relating to violence against Indian women;

"(H) support enforcement of tribal protection orders and implementation of full faith and credit educational projects and comity agreements between Indian tribes and States; and

"(I) ensure that adequate tribal technical assistance is made available to Indian tribes, tribal courts, tribal organizations, and tribal nonprofit organizations for all programs relating to violence against Indian women.

"(c) AUTHORITY.—

"(1) IN GENERAL.—The Deputy Director shall ensure that a portion of the tribal set-aside funds from any grant awarded under this Act, the Violence Against Women Act of 1994 (title IV of Public Law 103–322; 108 Stat. 1902), or the Violence Against Women Act of 2000 (division B of Public Law 106–386; 114 Stat. 1491) is used to enhance the capacity of Indian tribes to address the safety of Indian women.

"(2) ACCOUNTABILITY.—The Deputy Director shall ensure that some portion of the tribal set-aside funds from any grant made under this part is used to hold offenders accountable through—

"(A) enhancement of the response of Indian tribes to crimes of domestic violence, dating violence, sexual assault, and stalking against Indian women, including legal services for victims and Indian-specific offender programs;

"(B) development and maintenance of tribal domestic violence shelters or programs for battered Indian women, including sexual assault services, that are based upon the unique circumstances of the Indian women to be served;

"(C) development of tribal educational awareness programs and materials;

"(D) support for customary tribal activities to strengthen the intolerance of an Indian tribe to violence against Indian women; and

"(E) development, implementation, and maintenance of tribal electronic databases for tribal protection order registries.".

SEC. 908. ENHANCED CRIMINAL LAW RESOURCES.

(a) FIREARMS POSSESSION PROHIBITIONS.—Section 921(33)(A)(i) of title 18, United States Code, is amended to read: "(i) is a misdemeanor under Federal, State, or Tribal law; and".

(b) LAW ENFORCEMENT AUTHORITY.—Section 4(3) of the Indian Law Enforcement Reform Act (25 U.S.C. 2803(3) is amended—

(1) in subparagraph (A), by striking "or";

(2) in subparagraph (B), by striking the semicolon and inserting ", or"; and

(3) by adding at the end the following:

"(C) the offense is a misdemeanor crime of domestic violence, dating violence, stalking, or violation of a protection order and has, as an element, the use or attempted use of physical force, or the threatened use of a deadly weapon, committed by a current or former spouse, parent, or guardian of the victim, by a person with whom the victim shares a child in common, by a person who is cohabitating with or has cohabited with the victim as a spouse, parent, or guardian, or by a person similarly situated to a spouse, parent or guardian of the victim, and the employee has reasonable grounds to believe that the person to be arrested has committed, or is committing the crime;".

SEC. 909. DOMESTIC ASSAULT BY AN HABITUAL OFFENDER.

Chapter 7 of title 18, United States Code, is amended by adding at the end the following:

"§ 117. Domestic assault by an habitual offender

"(a) IN GENERAL.—Any person who commits a domestic assault within the special maritime and territorial jurisdiction of the United States or Indian country and who has a final conviction on at least 2 separate prior occasions in Federal, State, or Indian tribal court proceedings for offenses that would be, if subject to Federal jurisdiction—

"(1) any assault, sexual abuse, or serious violent felony against a spouse or intimate partner; or

"(2) an offense under chapter 110A,

shall be fined under this title, imprisoned for a term of not more than 5 years, or both, except that if substantial bodily injury results from violation under this section, the offender shall be imprisoned for a term of not more than 10 years.

"(b) DOMESTIC ASSAULT DEFINED.—In this section, the term 'domestic assault' means an assault committed by a current or former spouse, parent, child, or guardian of the victim, by a person with whom the victim shares a child in common, by a person who is cohabitating with or has cohabitated with the victim as a spouse, parent, child, or guardian, or by a person similarly situated to a spouse, parent, child, or guardian of the victim.".

TITLE X—DNA FINGERPRINTING

DNA Fingerprint
Act of 2005.

SEC. 1001. SHORT TITLE.

42 USC 13701
note.

This title may be cited as the "DNA Fingerprint Act of 2005".

SEC. 1002. USE OF OPT-OUT PROCEDURE TO REMOVE SAMPLES FROM NATIONAL DNA INDEX.

Section 210304 of the DNA Identification Act of 1994 (42 U.S.C. 14132) is amended—

(1) in subsection (a)(1)(C), by striking "DNA profiles" and all that follows through ", and";

(2) in subsection (d)(1), by striking subparagraph (A), and inserting the following:

Certification.

"(A) The Director of the Federal Bureau of Investigation shall promptly expunge from the index described in subsection (a) the DNA analysis of a person included in the index—

"(i) on the basis of conviction for a qualifying Federal offense or a qualifying District of Columbia offense (as determined under sections 3 and 4 of the DNA Analysis Backlog Elimination Act of 2000 (42 U.S.C. 14135a, 14135b), respectively), if the Director receives, for each conviction of the person of a qualifying offense,

PUBLIC LAW 109–271—AUG. 12, 2006

TECHNICAL CORRECTIONS TO
VIOLENCE AGAINST WOMEN AND DEPARTMENT OF
JUSTICE REAUTHORIZATION ACT OF 2005
Pages 763 – 766

TITLE IX—SAFETY FOR INDIAN WOMEN

(c) DEPORTABLE ALIENS.—Section 237(a)(1)(H)(ii) of such Act (8 U.S.C. 1227(a)(1)(H)(ii)) is amended to read as follows:
"(ii) is a VAWA self-petitioner.".

(d) REMOVAL.—Section 239(e)(2)(B) of such Act (8 U.S.C. 1229(e)(2)(B)) is amended by striking "(V)" and inserting "(U)".

(e) CANCELLATION OF REMOVAL.—Section 240A(b)(4)(B) of such Act (8 U.S.C. 1229b(b)(4)(B)) is amended by striking "they were applications filed under section 204(a)(1)(A)(iii), (A)(iv), (B)(ii), or (B)(iii) for purposes of section 245 (a) and (c)." and inserting "the applicants were VAWA self-petitioners.".

(f) ADJUSTMENT OF STATUS.—Section 245 of such Act (8 U.S.C. 1255) is amended—
(1) in subsection (a), by striking "under subparagraph (A)(iii), (A)(iv), (B)(ii), or (B)(iii) of section 204(a)(1) or" and inserting "as a VAWA self-petitioner"; and
(2) in subsection (c), by striking "under subparagraph (A)(iii), (A)(iv), (A)(v), (A)(vi), (B)(ii), (B)(iii), or (B)(iv) of section 204(a)(1)" and inserting "as a VAWA self-petitioner".

(g) IMMIGRATION OFFICERS.—Section 287 of such Act (8 U.S.C. 1357) is amended by redesignating subsection (i) as subsection (h).

(h) PENALTIES FOR DISCLOSURE OF INFORMATION.—Section 384(a)(2) of the Illegal Immigration Reform and Immigrant Responsibility Act of 1996 (8 U.S.C. 1367(a)(2)) is amended by striking "clause (iii) or (iv)" and all that follows and inserting "paragraph (15)(T), (15)(U), or (51) of section 101(a) of the Immigration and Nationality Act or section 240A(b)(2) of such Act.".

SEC. 7. TITLE IX—INDIAN WOMEN.

(a) OMNIBUS CRIME CONTROL AND SAFE STREETS.—
(1) GRANTS TO COMBAT VIOLENT CRIMES AGAINST WOMEN.—Part T of the Omnibus Crime Control and Safe Streets Act of 1968 is amended—
(A) by redesignating the second section 2007 (42 U.S.C. 3796gg–10) (relating to grants to Indian tribal governments), as added by section 906 of the Violence Against Women and Department of Justice Reauthorization Act of 2005, as section 2015;
(B) by redesignating the second section 2008 (42 U.S.C. 3796gg–11) (relating to a tribal deputy), as added by section 907 of the Violence Against Women and Department of Justice Reauthorization Act of 2005, as section 2016; and
(C) by moving those sections so as to appear at the end of the part.
(2) STATE GRANT AMOUNTS.—Section 2007(b) of the Omnibus Crime Control and Safe Streets Act of 1968 (42 U.S.C. 3796gg–1(b)), as amended by section 906(b) of the Violence Against Women and Department of Justice Reauthorization Act of 2005, is amended by striking paragraph (1) and inserting the following:
"(1) 10 percent shall be available for grants under the program authorized by section 2015, which shall not otherwise be subject to the requirements of this part (other than section 2008);".
(3) GRANTS TO INDIAN TRIBAL GOVERNMENTS.—Section 2015 of the Omnibus Crime Control and Safe Streets Act of 1968, as added by section 906 of the Violence Against Women and

168

Department of Justice Reauthorization Act of 2005 (as redesignated by paragraph (1)(A)), is amended—

42 USC
3796gg–10.

(A) in subsection (a)—

(i) in the matter preceding paragraph (1), by striking "and tribal organizations" and inserting "or authorized designees of Indian tribal governments";

(ii) in paragraph (6), by striking "and" at the end;

(iii) in paragraph (7), by striking the period at the end and inserting "; and"; and

(iv) by adding at the end the following:

"(8) provide legal assistance necessary to provide effective aid to victims of domestic violence, dating violence, stalking, or sexual assault who are seeking relief in legal matters arising as a consequence of that abuse or violence, at minimal or no cost to the victims."; and

(B) by striking subsection (c).

(4) TRIBAL DEPUTY RESPONSIBILITIES.—Section 2016(b)(1)(I) of the Omnibus Crime Control and Safe Streets Act of 1968

42 USC
3796gg–11.

(as redesignated by paragraph (1)(B)) is amended by inserting after "technical assistance" the following: "that is developed and provided by entities having expertise in tribal law, customary practices, and Federal Indian law".

(5) GRANTS TO ENCOURAGE ARREST POLICIES AND ENFORCEMENT OF PROTECTION ORDERS.—Section 2101 of the Omnibus Crime Control and Safe Streets Act of 1968 (42 U.S.C. 3796hh) is amended by striking subsection (e) and inserting the following:

"(e) ALLOTMENT FOR INDIAN TRIBES.—

"(1) IN GENERAL.—Not less than 10 percent of the total amount available under this section for each fiscal year shall be available for grants under the program authorized by section 2015.

"(2) APPLICABILITY OF PART.—The requirements of this part shall not apply to funds allocated for the program described in paragraph (1).".

(b) RURAL DOMESTIC VIOLENCE.—

(1) IN GENERAL.—Section 40295(d) of the Safe Homes for Women Act of 1994 (42 U.S.C. 13971(d)), as amended by section 306 of the Violence Against Women and Department of Justice Reauthorization Act of 2005, is amended by striking paragraph (1) and inserting the following:

"(1) ALLOTMENT FOR INDIAN TRIBES.—

"(A) IN GENERAL.—Not less than 10 percent of the total amount available under this section for each fiscal year shall be available for grants under the program authorized by section 2015 of the Omnibus Crime Control and Safe Streets Act of 1968 (42 U.S.C. 3796gg–10).

"(B) APPLICABILITY OF PART.—The requirements of this section shall not apply to funds allocated for the program described in subparagraph (A).".

(2) CONFORMING AMENDMENT.—Section 906 of the Violence Against Women and Department of Justice Reauthorization Act of 2005 is amended by—

42 USC 13971.
42 USC
3796gg–6, 10420,
13975.

(A) striking subsection (d); and

(B) redesignating subsections (e) through (g) as subsections (d) through (f), respectively.

(c) VIOLENCE AGAINST WOMEN ACT OF 1994.—

(1) TRANSITIONAL HOUSING ASSISTANCE.—Section 40299(g) of the Violence Against Women Act of 1994 (42 U.S.C. 13975(g)), as amended by sections 602 and 906 of the Violence Against Women and Department of Justice Reauthorization Act of 2005, is amended—

(A) in paragraph (3)(C), by striking clause (i) and inserting the following:

"(i) INDIAN TRIBES.—

"(I) IN GENERAL.—Not less than 10 percent of the total amount available under this section for each fiscal year shall be available for grants under the program authorized by section 2015 of the Omnibus Crime Control and Safe Streets Act of 1968 (42 U.S.C. 3796gg–10).

"(II) APPLICABILITY OF PART.—The requirements of this section shall not apply to funds allocated for the program described in subclause (I).";
and

(B) by striking paragraph (4).

(2) COURT TRAINING AND IMPROVEMENTS.—Section 41006 of the Violence Against Women Act of 1994 (42 U.S.C. 14043a–3), as added by section 105 of the Violence Against Women and Department of Justice Reauthorization Act of 2005, is amended by striking subsection (c) and inserting the following:

"(c) SET ASIDE.—

"(1) IN GENERAL.—Not less than 10 percent of the total amount available under this section for each fiscal year shall be available for grants under the program authorized by section 2015 of the Omnibus Crime Control and Safe Streets Act of 1968 (42 U.S.C. 3796gg–10).

"(2) APPLICABILITY OF PART.—The requirements of this section shall not apply to funds allocated for the program described in paragraph (1).".

(d) VIOLENCE AGAINST WOMEN ACT OF 2000.—

(1) LEGAL ASSISTANCE FOR VICTIMS.—Section 1201(f) of the Violence Against Women Act of 2000 (42 U.S.C. 3796gg–6(f)), as amended by sections 103 and 906 of the Violence Against Women and Department of Justice Reauthorization Act of 2005, is amended—

(A) in paragraph (2)—

(i) in subparagraph (A), by striking "10 percent" and inserting "3 percent";

(ii) by redesignating subparagraph (B) as subparagraph (C); and

(iii) by inserting after subparagraph (A) the following:

"(B) TRIBAL GOVERNMENT PROGRAM.—

"(i) IN GENERAL.—Not less than 7 percent of the total amount available under this section for each fiscal year shall be available for grants under the program authorized by section 2015 of the Omnibus Crime Control and Safe Streets Act of 1968 (42 U.S.C. 3796gg–10).

"(ii) APPLICABILITY OF PART.—The requirements of this section shall not apply to funds allocated for the program described in clause (i)."; and

(B) by striking paragraph (4).

(2) SAFE HAVENS FOR CHILDREN.—Section 1301 of the Violence Against Women Act of 2000 (42 U.S.C. 10420), as amended by sections 906 and 306 of the Violence Against Women and Department of Justice Reauthorization Act of 2005, is amended—
　(A) in subsection (e)(2)—
　　(i) by striking subparagraph (A); and
　　(ii) by redesignating subparagraphs (B) and (C) as subparagraphs (A) and (B), respectively; and
　(B) by striking subsection (f) and inserting the following:

"(f) ALLOTMENT FOR INDIAN TRIBES.—

Grants.

"(1) IN GENERAL.—Not less than 10 percent of the total amount available under this section for each fiscal year shall be available for grants under the program authorized by section 2015 of the Omnibus Crime Control and Safe Streets Act of 1968 (42 U.S.C. 3796gg–10).

"(2) APPLICABILITY OF PART.—The requirements of this section shall not apply to funds allocated for the program described in paragraph (1).".

SEC. 8. TITLE XI—DEPARTMENT OF JUSTICE.

(a) ORGANIZED RETAIL THEFT.—Section 1105(a)(3) of the Violence Against Women and Department of Justice Reauthorization Act of 2005 (28 U.S.C. 509 note) is amended by striking "The Attorney General through the Bureau of Justice Assistance in the Office of Justice may" and inserting "The Director of the Bureau of Justice Assistance of the Office of Justice Programs may".

20 USC 1152; 42 USC 3796gg–1, 3796gg–3, 10420, 13975, 14039.

(b) FORMULAS AND REPORTING.—Sections 1134 and 1135 of the Violence Against Women and Department of Justice Reauthorization Act of 2005 (Public Law 109–162; 119 Stat. 3108), and the amendments made by such sections, are repealed.

(c) GRANTS FOR YOUNG WITNESS ASSISTANCE.—Section 1136(a) of the Violence Against Women and Department of Justice Reauthorization Act of 2005 (42 U.S.C. 3743(a)) is amended by striking "The Attorney General, acting through the Bureau of Justice Assistance, may" and inserting "The Director of the Bureau of Justice Assistance of the Office of Justice Programs may".

(d) USE OF FEDERAL TRAINING FACILITIES.—Section 1173 of the Violence Against Women and Department of Justice Reauthorization Act of 2005 (28 U.S.C. 530c note) is amended—
　(1) in subsection (a), by inserting "or for meals, lodging, or other expenses related to such internal training or conference meeting" before the period; and
　(2) in subsection (b), by striking "that requires specific authorization" and inserting "authorized".

(e) OFFICE OF AUDIT, ASSESSMENT, AND MANAGEMENT.—Part A of title I of the Omnibus Crime Control and Safe Streets Act of 1968 (42 U.S.C. 3711 et seq.) is amended by redesignating the section 105 titled "**OFFICE OF AUDIT, ASSESSMENT, AND MANAGEMENT**" as section 109 and transferring such section to the end of such part A.

42 USC 3712d, 3712h.

(f) COMMUNITY CAPACITY DEVELOPMENT OFFICE.—Section 106 of the Omnibus Crime Control and Safe Streets Act of 1968 (42 U.S.C. 3712e) is amended by striking "section 105(b)" each place such term appears and inserting "section 103(b)".

Cover Design:

"Reclaiming Our Power"
Shan Goshorn
2014
16" X 16" X 13.5"
Arches watercolor paper splints printed with archival inks, acrylic paint

The interior of this double-weave basket is woven with high statistics of violence directed at Indian women on tribal lands by non-Natives. These facts include: "3 out of 4 Native women will be physically assaulted in their lifetime, Native women are 10 times more likely to be murdered than any other group of women, 1 in 3 Native women will be raped in their lifetime, and 88% of crimes against Indian women are by non-natives but tribal courts have ZERO authority to prosecute them." The paper text is washed with purple, black and blue paint to emphasize the severity of this violence. The exterior is woven with the language in Sections 904, 905, and 910 of the reauthorization of the Violence Against Women Act (VAWA) of 2013. This language recognizes the inherent right of tribes to protect Indian women who suffer specific abuse by non-Natives on tribal lands. Prior to the enactment of this law, non-Natives could act without fear of prosecution for these crimes. Many thanks to the brave women and men who worked tirelessly, including their public testimony of personal accounts which convinced the House and Senate of the need for this legislation. Their testimonies are literally what passed the vote.

It was important to me for this basket to be a community project, so I sent out an e-request and received responses from more than 50 Native women from across the Northern Hemisphere. I requested images of women wearing street clothes (to indicate how violence happens at any time, not just at powwows) and for females of all ages (to show how this can happen to our daughters, our sisters, our mothers, our grandmothers, our friends). I obscured individual faces to illustrate the anonymity of the victims and pervasiveness of this violence. All the figures are wrapped in intertribal shawls, metaphorically indicating how the new provisions in this Act will serve to wrap around us like a protective shield and untie the hands of tribal courts to dispense justice.

Made in the USA
San Bernardino, CA
03 April 2015